AWARE OF THE MOUNTAIN

Mountaineering as Yoga

Gil Parker

To Bill & Joan,
who have already learned much
of this, intuitively.
Gil.

To Dave, who led all the hard routes,

And Jean, who showed me the way to yoga.

"It is like my life, which runs its course and I know neither its start nor its conclusion." *Kurt Diemberger*

"If he is indeed wise he does not bid you enter the house of his wisdom, but rather leads you to the threshold of your own mind." *Kahlil Gibran*

National Library of Canada Cataloguing in Publication Data

Parker, Gil
Aware of the mountain : mountaineering as yoga

ISBN 1-55212-965-9

1. Parker, Gil 2. Mountaineering. 3. Yoga, Hatha 4. Self-realization. I. Title.

GV199.92.P37A3 2001 796.52'2'092 C2001-903055-X

TRAFFORD

This book was published *on-demand* in cooperation with Trafford Publishing.
On-demand publishing is a unique process and service of making a book available for retail sale to the public taking advantage of on-demand manufacturing and Internet marketing. **On-demand publishing** includes promotions, retail sales, manufacturing, order fulfilment, accounting and collecting royalties on behalf of the author.

Suite 6E, 2333 Government St., Victoria, B.C. V8T 4P4, CANADA
Phone 250-383-6864 Toll-free 1-888-232-4444 (Canada & US)
Fax 250-383-6804 E-mail sales@trafford.com
Web site www.trafford.com TRAFFORD PUBLISHING IS A DIVISION OF TRAFFORD HOLDINGS LTD.
Trafford Catalogue #01-0367 www.trafford.com/robots/01-0367.html

10 9 8 7 6 5 4 3 2

AWARE OF THE MOUNTAIN
Mountaineering as Yoga

Gil Parker

CONTENTS

PHOTOGRAPHS

All other photos by author

FOREWORD by Sandy Briggs

It is wonderful and easy in the effervescence of youth to stand on a high sunny summit and fling one's arms skyward in sheer unself-conscious joy. It is even more wonderful when such joy accompanies one through the seasons of a long and active life.

But anyone for whom the climbing of mountains evolves from a casual interest into a long-term passion is sooner or later faced with a number of engaging questions. These arise partly from a natural desire to defend this passion--to justify it to others--and partly from the tendency of all thinking people to ponder the significance of their own lives, or the significance of life itself.

Probably few mountaineers delude themselves with the notion that all the possible motives for climbing mountains are good--indeed most passions are selfish in some way--or that all people who climb mountains are good. Nevertheless the question poses itself as to whether mountaineering might in some way be special among human activities. In attempting to defend a positive response to this question one must think carefully about the value of mountaineering and about its values. Certainly mountaineering has spawned a large, often introspective, and occasionally inspirational literature. The metaphor of climbing a mountain as a difficult and noble act occurs across the spectrum of human endeavour from play and business to love and war.

Further questioning arises in the search for meaning in the face of injury or death in the mountains. We all know that life has risks. However, our modern society has successfully insulated us from so many of these risks that, in some respects, the insulation is too great. We have, in large measure, lost the intense feeling of freedom and of being alive that comes when we assume higher levels of responsibility for our own actions, and this may explain much of the recent surge in popularity of activities involving both skill and risk. Probably most mountaineers acknowledge the existence of blind luck, and there are few who have been at the game for any length of time who do not have tales of close calls or sad stories of friends who have died in the mountains. Yet risk is a part of the formula. One could argue that the true tragedies are cases in which a climber is injured or killed in a situation involving a level of risk higher than that which he/she personally accepted at that time. Years ago I began to question the extent to which we are justified in criticizing those climbers who accept high risks and who are thereby killed.

The pioneer Scottish mountaineer W. H. Murray has written that "Prudence is not a goddess to be worshipped, least of all in youth: or sea and air would yet be unnavigated, no man ever have shared his last crust, or climbed a mountain."

But let us not be trapped by the illusion of glory. Australian mountaineer Greg Child has commented eloquently on risk in mountaineering: "There is a state of mind that sometimes infests climbers in which the end result achieves a significance beyond anything that the future may hold. For a few minutes or hours you cast aside all that had previously been held as worth living for, and you focus on one risky move or stretch of ground which becomes the only thing that ever mattered. This state of mind is what is both fantastic and reckless about the game. Since everything is at stake in these moments, you had better be sure to recognize them and have no illusions about what lies on the other side of luck."

Many mountaineers have written accounts of their expeditions, and many of these author-climbers have tried to analyse as well as describe the people and events involved. It is the rare mountaineer who has taken pen in hand to describe the integration of mountaineering into his own life and philosophy, to pursue lessons and the connections among all the different aspects, such as relationships, work, play, and spirituality, which give life substance and meaning.

It is rarer when an experienced mountaineer really tries to help us understand the long answers to the questions mentioned above. That's because it isn't easy. That's because the writing of a book, especially a thoughtful and personal book, is comparable to an arduous mountaineering adventure. This book is a look into that adventure for those of you who seek the long answers, and I know that you will profit from the expedition at hand. Good climbing!

Alexander G. (Sandy) Briggs,
Mountaineer and Arctic Explorer

Climbing a mountain, whether an excursion to a local crag or an expedition to a foreign range, is a series of actions and events which together make up a journey. It is also an array of thoughts, about what we see, what we are doing, and how we are feeling inside. But it goes beyond all that, encompassing the memories, solitary or shared, of the climb, the people who came along, the difficulties and pleasures and, perhaps, the lessons learned.

Very few mountaineers start climbing to find out something about life. They may study techniques for ascending glaciers or various types of rock, systems to protect the leader in the event of a fall, or, how to predict weather from the appearance of clouds. Few expect to learn about their own personality, their relationship with their mother or partner, their reactions to physical conditions or stress. And almost none would expect to find a philosophy of life, or a belief in a personal or universal spirituality. Too often, we move from action to action without reflecting, thus losing the greater value of living.

Yet, those who have climbed over an extended period will verify that they have garnered elements of all of these aspects of life. In my own case, discoveries usually occurred long after the climb itself. Owing to a happy combination of interests and circumstances my life has had a strong element of serendipity. A love of nature tugged me into the outdoors, a restless nature pushed me to climb and a questioning mentality drew me towards the spiritual aspect of mountaineering.

Although my early religious training had included both the United Church of Canada (to mollify my mother) and the Anglican church (where I held a janitorial job for a matronly nun) I abandoned formal religion when I left my 'teens. I agreed with Karl Marx when he called religion "the opiate of the people."

My early love of nature may have developed from a rural upbringing. Later, with the rigours of family and job pressing upon me, I was thrust into questioning the way I reacted to other people and situations, searching for my own understanding of life's meaning. Therefore, the spirituality to which I was attracted was not very subtle. I found a form of learning which was called yoga, so completely grounded in dealing with the matters of daily life that it meshed with my practical nature as well as with the mystical sport of mountaineering.

This is the story of some of the milestones on my path. Mountaineering is an essential part of my life and my yoga is a way of better understanding the climbs, of seeing life as a total entity. I have never climbed mountains with the singular ambition necessary to achieve fame in the alpine world. Something else in my conscious and sub-conscious mind draws me to the high hills. Of course, adventure has a way of finding anyone who frequents remote regions. Some time after the specific journeys, and not in any formal way, the lessons of those climbs came clearer to me. I would not deny such intuitive experiences to anyone.

I have chosen to write this book as an autobiography, recording some of my milestones and even epiphanies. While my chosen highway was mountaineering and my vehicle yoga, the experiences could relate to many different activities, physical or otherwise. But mountaineering is such an apt metaphor for life, and yoga a discipline of increased awareness, that the two fit perfectly for me. Taken a step beyond the simple exercises and relaxation techniques, yoga study can provide increased philosophical clarity and mystical unity.

Unity with what? With God? Or, using my own definition of God, I mean unity with my untapped inner resources, with a power within me that I can reach. As reader, you may wish to define such progress simply as mental and emotional satisfaction.

I can identify some step-by-step progress in my own life. But it would require an egocentric focus to catalogue such indefinite results. And that progression has not always happened. So, this book is not written in a prescriptive, self-help format. My purpose, via this book, will be complete if you find even a few tools for your own search within my story.

"The Bird of Time has but a little way to fly—and lo! the Bird is on the Wing." *Rubaiyat of Omar Khayyam.*

For prairie boys, years of living on flatlands with scrub brush and wheat fields stretching beyond imagination eastward gave us a healthy respect for anything higher than a house. We knew that streams and rivers cut sizeable valleys, but they were always cut downward from the reference plane, *the flatland.* At the western edge of our world, the Rockies presented a different boundary, a visual barrier to travel and to our psychology. True, there were passes threaded by roads and railways, but most of these needed the protection of tunnels and avalanche sheds. Even so, winter snow slides would close the routes to the west coast. This was indeed, like Maurice Herzog's wall of rock and ice on the north side of Mount Annapurna; it was our *Grande Barrier!*

Growing up as the youngest of five, a distant four years behind my brother, Ken, was excuse enough to become an insecure, introverted, self-centred teen. As a confirmed bookworm, I dreamed myself into all of my books, from the cowboy romances of Zane Grey to the travels of Halliburton and Durrell. Not surprising then, that Herzog transported me from the rhododendron valleys of Nepal to the mysterious snowfields of Dhaulagiri and Annapurna. I redrew all of his book's expedition maps, even fabricated my own crampons from tacks and old boot soles, sewed together with straps and buckles. On the terrain of Alberta's northern parkland there were no steep hills to test them; luckily they were lost to some forgotten attic. Little did I know, then, that I would eventually climb in those same mountains, retracing part of Herzog's solo journey to Manang. Nor could I, in those early years, expect to learn a code of living, born in nearby reaches of India and Tibet and carried down the ages as the practice of yoga.

Living near Peace River town in Alberta, I was a long way from those Rocky Mountains. Both of my parents taught in a two room schoolhouse of a small farming village. I was the only child in the family still left at home. My oldest brother, Bill, having left the army after the war, was working on an engineering degree, while both of my sisters were studying to become teachers. Ken, nearest in age to me, lived with the girls in a basement suite near the university in Edmonton, delivering groceries by bicycle to help with the food money. He finished what he could stomach of high school, then left for the west coast of British Columbia, where he ran a small Hudson's Bay Company trading post.

This left me alone on the school ground. All the other students (but one) in the village could speak Ukrainian, and did. My sole companion was Rene, the son of the French Canadian section master for our part of the Northern Alberta Railway. After Ken sent me a .22 Cooey single-shot rifle for Christmas, Rene and I spent hours tramping the snowy bushland, shooting prairie chickens and rabbits, essential meat for our families' tables.

With my parents' focus on school academics, often I was alone. My bookishness isolated me from my fellows but also won me a way into the mountains. For an essay about oil prospecting in the North, I won a summer scholarship to Banff's "School of Fine Arts", as it was then called. As a thirteen year old, I had six weeks surrounded by rock and snow peaks, my imagination whetted by artists, dancers, musicians and by the twenty-odd adult writers in my classes.

Lacking supervision by my parents, I neglected the writing assignments and struck off for the outdoors. Hitch-hiking to Johnston's Canyon, we climbed above the falls into the spectacular Sawback Range. We followed animal trails up the valley and sat staring for an hour at boiling quicksand in the depths of a crystal clear pool, later to become a tourist destination, the "Inkpots." On Sulphur Mountain, we climbed at night to be there to see the sunrise over the prairies. Basil and I lobbed pebbles ahead into the bush to scare the girls in the party. Their shrieks frightened off any threats, real or imagined, and we reached the old teahouse on the summit at 3 a.m., long before the sun was due. We invited our girlfriends (who were sort of communal at that stage) to pass the chilly hour or two in a field of heather, sheltered from the dew by stunted cedars. One was about to be married. Surprisingly, she was rather the more forward, and we formed a warm and sleepless party.

In this situation and others, my adaptability to new situations was often lacking. That summer I learned other people games, social games, competitive games between performers, status games among the writers of my class. But the writers at least analysed character and motive, awakening my first significant introspection.

Basil, my violinist roommate, and I went alone on our next outing, an attempt on Mount Rundle. Only slightly less of a novice than me, he gambolled up the ridge and half way up a cliff which soon became more than our skills could handle. Dealing with our vertigo, climbing down with no rope, was much harder. Then, we found a traverse below the cliff band and a laid-back gully giving access to the upper mountain. After a struggle up interminable scree, we arrived at the wrong summit! But it was nearly as high as the main peak and towered over the Bow River Valley. Peering over the edge, I felt my stomach rise in my throat. Two thousand metres of air above the golf course fairways. I was hooked.

After high school I tried the Canadian Navy. I found that the sea was exciting but the military (group) discipline was not. Gunner Smith seemed to enjoy intimidating young cadets. I escaped most of the punishment dealt to the more adventurous of my class, until one day I gave the wrong command during drill exercises and marched the platoon into the side of the barracks. Perhaps my classmates forgave me the 5 a.m. drill practice that the Gunner prescribed; I did not. The theory was that we would remember our errors. But, I could not accept a code whereby others were punished for my mistakes, or vice versa.

There were good times, too: playing rugby against a Vancouver private school, rowing and sailing in Esquimalt harbour, training and competing in cross-country races. The primitive life of rural Alberta stood me in good stead here; the Royal Roads course was similar to the rabbit trapline that I had run in all seasons, even in deep winter snows.

The cruise on H.M.C.S. Ontario was formative for me. I inspected London and Portsmouth with Leonard, a high school chum who had joined the Navy with me. On leave in Scotland, we played golf at the "Royal and Ancient" course in Saint Andrews. We bought bikes and toured both banks of the Firth of Forth. For the romantics in our shipboard class, Copenhagen, and especially Tivoli, was the “mecca”. I was stuck with duty-watch aboard ship and left that port, uneducated and unscathed.

The ship sailed the Kattegat to Oslo where a party was arranged by our embassy. All of the cadets of my division arrived at a two storey mansion in the suburbs where we were welcomed by young hostesses from a local girls' school. They had volunteered for the job and clearly took their duties seriously. We ate, drank non-alcoholic punch and danced to records of the fifties. With no common language, conversation was limited. Sometime in the later hours, Helga's eyes brightened, remembering a phrase, “make love to me!” Shy perhaps, but always a good student, I took that as an invitation, only to find she merely knew the name of the song Jo Stafford was singing. Still, the end of the evening came too soon. When we parted, we were both very sad.

Now I understood the cloud that hung over the boys in our mess when the ship had sailed from Copenhagen. Helga had done for my self-confidence what Gunner Smith never could do.

At the end of my compulsory time, I quit the Navy, took the train from Vancouver to Banff, uncrated my bike and headed for Edmonton via Jasper. The "Columbia Parkway" did not yet exist. The road was much more of a challenge than it is today, with unpaved sections over Bow Pass and a bare minimum of camping facilities. But the mountains were white and shining beacons. I rested in the ditches, planning rock routes up unknown strata, tracing lines around glacial snouts to the upper snowfields where the view--well, it must be incredible! But east of Jasper there was road construction and the fall rainstorms made it difficult for a bike.

After two long days I stumbled into my parent's house on Edmonton's south side, not knowing my next move. It was September; my oldest brother, Bill, was entering his final year in engineering. With the tuition fee left by my parents (who were teaching in a nearby town) and a room in the basement, I started the long four year grind toward a similar goal. The assimilation of facts, often useless (calculus), sometimes irrelevant (jet engine laboratory), was a distinct challenge. To be able to retain enough to pass the required examinations occupied all waking hours for eight months of the year. During summers, surveying the untracked arctic tundra for the Topographic Survey of Canada was welcome relief.

As student support for the Ottawa-based surveyors, my job was seldom technical, but often required me to do my work alone in remote wilderness. Usually, our "Beaver" aircraft would land on a lake, dropping me on shore to find my way to the mountaintop circled on an aerial photograph. Once there I would clear a landing spot for the helicopter and set up a marker over a metal survey plug drilled into the rock. A hike back to the lake, or a ride down in the chopper while the surveyor read the angles, completed my work. On one occasion, neither plane came. The helicopter had some mechanical failure and crash landed; the Beaver was out searching. I crouched in a ball, trying to avoid being eaten alive by mosquitoes, for most of the long arctic night. Finally, in the early hours of the twilight morning, the Beaver flew over, wagged its wings and landed on a nearby lake.

There were also days when the fog socked in, keeping the planes grounded, days I would roam the tundra, often finding huge herds of caribou, migrating. I played cowboy, isolating a dozen or so, then chasing them across the uneven ground for an hour, till we both gave up, standing face-to-face, our breath steaming in the cool, wet air. As the summers passed I learned to take care of myself in the wilds, learned to respect those places and the animals that lived there.

Two years after graduation, I was back in the Rockies, working on a highway bridge over Nigel Creek, in the deep mountains just south of the Columbia Icefields. It was below Parker's Ridge where, in summer, the mountain goats bounded from ledge to ledge and, in winter, the "telemark" skiers climbed for powder snow. South of our camp was the Weeping Wall, a hangout for ice climbers. But I was still unaware of these pursuits, still getting started in a profession, still starting to build a family.

Jean and I had dated on the ski slopes of Mount Norquay. We actually were a grade apart in the same school in Peace River town before my Navy days; her mother was my English and social studies teacher. Partly because I always travelled by schoolbus in the morning, home again right after classes, we never had spoken. But the Navy, university and construction-site living reduced my reticence, gave me the confidence to try. She was beautiful, with a physical lightness that fascinated me. When she walked, it was with the angular grace of a walking deer, about to burst into flight. But it was the quality of our communication that was unique. Often it did not involve verbal expression; I had no experience of anything else. It was mysterious, exciting, but often frustrating. I did not understand what was meant by intuition, by empathy. Even then I must have foreseen a long period of learning. That she found me of interest amazed me; our chemistry was certainly working.

We honeymooned in the red-roofed and friendly Icefields Chalet. Our holidays were a series of ski weeks in the mountains. We were building a life together: home, professions and, before long, one baby boy--then another. For my work as a bridge engineer, more professional challenges presented themselves. We moved to Victoria on Vancouver Island, for me, a new employer. For Jean, it meant leaving her nursing profession to ride herd on two small boys, a new life with few friends in an unfamiliar place.

It is clear to me now that I was a classic *type A* personality, focused on trying every opportunity, not content to waste time on introspection. With the children roaming our lives, little time was left for learning, let alone philosophy.

The mountains were still peripheral to my vision. I assumed it was an exclusive sport for a special breed, the Herzogs and the Hillarys. Since most of my mountain knowledge had come from adventure books, I little suspected that there was a vast body of climbers who never aspired to the Himalayas or even the difficult climbs of the Rockies. But when my friends Fred and Murray first enticed me into the peaks across Juan de Fuca Strait, Mount Olympus caught my attention.

It was just a weekend trip from the Hot Springs to Appleton Pass. Above the springs the valley reeked of skunk cabbage. The humming silence, like a distant buzzing of yellow jackets in the salal, was the noise of the wilderness.

The trail, rising steadily westward, was spongy on centuries of dropped fir needles. Then, turning south, we spotted half a dozen Roosevelt elk on a treeless promontory. They saw us also. All through the long, hot afternoon the elk increased the space between us, disappearing over the bare ground of the pass. Two hours later we reached the same point. The effort had been considerable for out-of-condition novices.

Fred erected our thirty dollar, hardware-store tent. It had a floor that lasted two summers and grommets that tore out in the first storm. But that evening it sheltered us from the dew. Mountains stretched along the south horizon, from The Needles in the east, the slender black pinnacles marching away from Mt Constance, right around to the west ridges fading into the Pacific. Dominating everything was Mount Olympus, proudly rising above the dark green timbered hills of the Soleduck valley to the south. Its lower reaches were blocked from view; the peak floated with no apparent connection to the Earth.

Through the rising ocean fog the sun's last rays filtered, touching the milky shoulders of Mount Olympus; the mountain's white cape blushed pink, darkened to rose, then grey. Somewhere in the memories from that day, Olympus formed my beginning companionship with the mountains.

Yoga struck my conscious mind when I was in my thirties. A front page photo in our newspaper showed Pierre Trudeau, then an aspirant to lead Canada, demonstrating his ability to do "mayurasana", the peacock pose. If this proud and stylish bird was his symbol, some would say that Trudeau had chosen a perfect example. But it was not an easy show-off pose. Balanced on his hands, his horizontal body poised above the floor, he held his entire weight suspended only on his elbows tucked into his rigid solar plexus.

Hatha yoga classes were taught at the YM/YWCA. I began to use yoga to complement the aerobics of distance running and the hard physical work of climbing. But, the instructor did not want me running before the yoga classes. "You have all of your blood in the muscles; we want it in the joints." There was only one lunch hour and I wanted to run to keep up my training. So I ran and cut yoga.

Later, I found another class. Betty Neare was willing to accommodate my idiosyncrasies. She assumed that eventually the benefits of yoga would draw me into more and detailed practice. She was right. Within a year I was teaching my own Hatha Yoga classes at the YMCA, mostly directed towards men, men who had hitherto avoided yoga as a "sissy sport." These sessions were still just exercise classes. While I copied and taught the same relaxation practices I learned from other instructors, I avoided anything that might have been considered "spiritual." I doubted that the several businessmen who came to the "Y" would stay, especially if what I did was construed as something religious—even something based on non-Christian origins. More than that, I was not prepared to teach beyond the asanas, the basic yogic postures. I did not understand then, that even the Hatha yoga postures are part of a practice that tries to integrate mind, body and spirit. That would come later.

It was Jean who shocked me into looking at a wider view of yoga. She booked into the summer session at the Yasodhara Ashram in the Kootenay region of British Columbia, and took our two boys along for their holidays. It was apparent that she was starting to look seriously at the spiritual side of yoga. I took her attendance there as an implicit threat to the status quo. I was shocked by the idea that anyone (me, for example) would need to get into discussions of philosophy or examine spiritual beliefs as a route to altering my personal behaviour. But there was an implication that our relationship needed attention, that we might not be able to sort out all our difficulties simply by discussing them. Besides, I was not too good at those kinds of deep discussions.

I visited the ashram many times that summer, despite the meagre holidays my job permitted. The boys thrived in the rural atmosphere, helping with the garden and orchard, exploring art and games with other children, swimming at South Beach or the hot springs. But it was not a holiday for most of the adults. They laboured over the meaning of love, work, relationships, and, as it was an implicit component of all of these, their spirituality. This yoga consisted primarily of discussion workshops, philosophical papers, and techniques for working through life problems--health, personality and feelings--by what was called "spiritual practice."

So, with a more committing kind of yoga looming, I slowly became involved in ashram life. With the background of Hatha yoga and a vital interest in what my partner was getting into, it was easy to become immersed. As a typical yoga-spouse, so common of the fringes of ashram activity, I found that I really didn't know what was going on. I felt threatened, that our marriage was perhaps the subject of intense scrutiny by others in the workshops. The fact was, most of the couples that were there had marital problems; most were in process of breaking up. It didn't help that residents were friendly, sympathetic and willing to involve me in other aspects of ashram life.

Initially, I was simply on a holiday. I swam with our two boys, worked a bit in the farm that supplied vegetables and dairy products for residents and guests. As an engineer, I helped to design a new building that was needed. But mostly, I did Hatha yoga regularly every morning, read about yoga, listened to lectures in the evenings and went to satsang, an evening prayer meeting of chanting and meditation. Despite the tasty meals that were served in the dining room, I went on a five day fast which was rumoured to help all sorts of ills, perhaps my own life-long sinus condition. On the fifth day without solid food I drove to the north end of Kokanee Park and hiked 800 metres up the Bridal Veil Falls trail. Descending, with a hat full of berries seeping magenta through my white sunhat, I was actually able to breathe without obstruction. The world had an effervescent glow. Unfortunately, it was only a temporary relief.

Jean and I discussed the teachings she was hearing, talked about the papers she had to write. I couldn't fathom where these were leading. She was in a different space. In "Practical Yoga" by Ernest Wood, the author discusses the yoga of Pantanjali, an Indian who lived about the second century B.C. He identifies three reasons for studying yoga. Much simplified, these are:

to make life richer and stronger,

to expand psychic powers and search for realms beyond earth, and,

to solve the mystery of life—the "why are we here?"—the deeper purposes of existence.

I wasn't particularly interested in anything beyond the first, the improvement of life here on earth! No one could ignore such benefits, or even perhaps, to speculate on the meaning of life. As for the occult, Jean was fascinated by discussions of mystical powers of famous yogis, even some who visited the ashram, but that was just curiosity. For both of us, the focus was the here-and-now.

In fact, the exercises and workshops of Jean's courses seemed to be more concerned with personality, with understanding character weaknesses, emotional prejudices and egotistic biases. This approach to self-understanding was foreign to me. As with any new idea, it involved the non-attachment to previous beliefs, in effect, a non-judgmental surrendering to whatever was happening.

Collectively, this way of thinking was totally opposite

to my life experience to date. But eventually, it allowed me to step back from the yoga itself, to look at what was happening in our daily life and, for me, in my mountaineering. Parallels occurred in the way we taught climbing courses, or how we dealt with personality differences in the climbing parties. The work of yoga required tremendous discipline and was in many ways as committing as backing over a cliff to rappel down a mountain. Another parallel to climbing that occurred to me early on was whether to study under a specific guru—like a decision to climb with a particular mountain guide. These ideas started to infiltrate other regions of my daily life.

"With all I can do to save my own life every day, still there's this fear of showing fear." *Sid Marty*

Hostility and resentment point to ego, to self-importance."
Swami Sivananda Rahda

About the same time I joined the Alpine Club of Canada. As it turned out, I was beginning a life adventure with the mountains and with climbers and their sport. Mountaineers were a queer cross-section when viewed from the outside, but I got to know a lot of them very quickly. They exhibited all of the human foibles that may be found in any other group, but while focused on their climbing, these characteristics came into luminous clarity.

Milan Jelensky was employed to teach the Alpine Club's mountaineering course, through several lectures staged at a community college, and later, with help from amateur climbers on the rocks west of Victoria. He was grizzled and worn in body, but had an ironical sense of humour, common to many mountaineers.

Jelensky taught the whole gamut of a mountain traveller's skills in a sterile classroom atmosphere: how to plan your pack, how to cross a glacial torrent, how to use compass and altimeter and, finally, the more technical aspects of the sport. These included "belays" (ways to protect a rope leader's fall) how to cut steps in steep ice, or how to extract a fallen buddy from a crevasse. The "Bible" for the course was a book entitled "The Freedom of the Hills," and Milan inspired everyone to gain that freedom. He never bragged of his own successes on incredible routes, but you knew he'd been there. Even with Jelensky there was this studied understatement. For each climber there is always a class of climbers better, or more adventurous.

Understatement becomes a hedge against that higher class. Climbers usually start using this device while yet a novice and, by habit, carry it on through many years of experimenting with much more difficult snow and rock routes.

Adam Johnston was our other early mentor. He was a rock-climber who wouldn't climb anything inaccessible by car. And if Milan was helpful and cajoling, Adam was challenging and mocking. His indisputable ability on rock created an invincible aura, his naked, barrel chest and blond hair reinforcing his god-like demeanour.

Especially with gullible beginners, Adam never missed a chance to grandstand; he often climbed above the boat-launching ramp at Fleming Beach where boaters and urban walkers assured him of a gaping audience. Modest, he was not, but a magnet to our group. Every Tuesday night after work, six or eight of us would gather at the cliffs along Humpback Road west of Victoria, wolf down 'burgers and 'shakes, tie on body harnesses, arrange our slings and anchor equipment, then hike up to the bottom of the face. There we would practise rope handling, experience the void beneath our feet and, as Adam said, learn to deal "only with what you can reach with your hands and feet."

Our practice sessions on the local crags provided technique, but little understanding of the real processes of mountaineering. Our notes on back-packing were of some help, but there was nothing that taught you to leave extra gear at home as well as having to carry it over rough terrain for many long hours. My classroom lessons on step-cutting on ice began to be integrated after I had cut a hundred metres up a steep face on Mount Schoen. Descending later, it became clear why two steps were always cut at the same level. For stability during down-climbing, these techniques had to become automatic.

It was the same with people. You had to study them

in action. The crucible of extreme fatigue and fear was the true testing ground. There we learned the strengths and the failings of our companions, and of ourselves. Then, we could criticize or applaud our teachers; we could emulate them, or learn to do better.

After receiving instruction from Jelensky and Johnston and with limited experience climbing in the easy peaks near Buttle Lake, we agreed to teach a fundamental course for the YMCA. In retrospect, I believe we were naive, but justified our bravado by careful practice of systems and choosing easy routes for the students. To bring the classes to a practical conclusion, we organized a two day outing west of Nanaimo, on Vancouver Island.

On our objective, Mount Arrowsmith, we had tried several times to find an easy route. We knew that there was one somewhere--everyone we talked to said they had climbed the peak. Our Arrowsmith siege continued over some years. Access to the upper part of the mountain was difficult then; the usual trip involved a day hike up to Cokely Mountain, over its rocky top to a col. From this saddle we tried every gully on Arrowsmith's north face; in one we found twisted metal and nickels and dimes from an unknown airplane crash, in the next, a microwave repeater station the wind had blown off the ridge, and in the third, after a long, dangerous climb, a natural "chockstone" blocked our progress. We had to come down, like my earlier Mount Rundle experience, with precious few holds. But, at least, with a rope!

After Jelensky opened our eyes to elementary techniques we discovered an easier way. Just follow the path up the right hand ridge, stay out of the gullies and traverse the bumps on the top. There was really only one problem left--the exposed, near vertical ridge of the final tower, or the steep snow chute to its right.

Loggers had cut a swath of timber above Cameron Lake and reduced our long, forested approach hike to a bumpy car ride on a one lane dirt road. Leaving the cars at the old Rousseau cabin, we wound our way up the creek to the col. The saddle between the rocky face of Cokely and the bluffs of Arrowsmith was a funnel for ocean breezes channelled up the Alberni Canal. We chose the campsite on the lee slope out of the direct wind. On the harder, remnant spring snow we practised our iceaxe self-arrests. Each student slid down the slope, then dropped onto the iceaxe shaft, burying the pick and stopping the slide.

The next morning we started early. Peter and Bob, as my co-instructors, arranged the team into three ropes at the base of the ridge. There was no real climbing, but in several places the route passed above a sharp drop. I recalled my earlier attempts on the gullies and was careful that none of our novice climbers would get "psyched out" on their first real mountain. And, of course, we all needed rope-handling experience.

As we approached the steep north ridge of the final tower, my stomach began to do flips. This looked much harder than the reports indicated. The climbing route was straight forward, but to our left the tower dropped-off hundreds of metres into a dark cirque. To the right, our line of climbing would be along a cliff edge, 100 metres above the snowfield. Here was a place to concentrate only on the reach of your hands and feet and ignore the great nothingness below.

"There is no objective danger," I told myself, "just control your own psyche." This was not the place to worry aloud for the trainees to hear.

We noticed a lone hiker approaching over the bumps behind us. As we arranged our hardware for the final assault he caught us up, nodded as he passed and proceeded to climb straight up the tower without the benefit of a rope!

"Hey, Gil. Why don't you tie onto 'High-pockets Harry' there?" quipped Bob, who was concerned--even more than I--

about the pitch ahead. I didn't trust myself a response; rather, I started off, keeping to the centre of the ridge. There was no technical difficulty, only exposure to the void on either side.

Starting onto the last vertical section, I followed 'Harry's' route around a rock projection onto a ledge. The holds were obvious but the stance precarious. An angle-shaped piton went into a crack with clear, ringing blows, the sound of security. I connected the rope to the piton with a carabiner, a link similar to a chain link, but having a spring-loaded side gate. With the rope sliding free, controlled by my belayer, I felt much more relaxed. 'Harry' had just down-climbed the face above me, passing me on the ledge. In limited English he explained that he was Danish, from a freighter docked in the town below, loading pulp from the mill at Port Alberni. He was clearly comfortable in high places and scampered on down past my rope, past Bob's and then Peter's. Perhaps as a result of this display, but more likely because they were also concerned about the exposure of the route, Bob now tied onto the tail of my rope, Peter to his, and we continued as an extended 150 m roped party. Canada may never have seen such a sight, one more usual in Russia where everyone traditionally climbs on the same rope. Everyone, or no one, makes it.

Above the ledge the holds were thin and the cliff fell away behind me to a dark void. Half way up the cliff I felt a shadow cover me, heard a strange swoosh of air, as from a giant eagle's wings. I glanced up, and nearly let go of my holds. Not far above was a glider, rising on the thermals, hugging the tower's face.

Swearing, I lunged for the bush at the top of the crack. I looped a nylon sling around its small but sturdy trunk. Vegetation has such a comfortable feel! I was now on easier, sloping rock that led up to the summit and, thankfully, the glider was gone. Sitting anchored "on belay," I took in rope, securing each climber as he or she mounted the steep cliff and moved away from the exposed face.

The summit yielded a mixture of relief and the pleasure of magnificent scenery in all directions. The Pacific was our western horizon. To the south east, the parade of volcanoes: Baker, Glacier Peak and Mount Rainier. Then, we strained our imagination northward through the afternoon haze towards a white tip, a peak that we knew must be Mount Waddington. If the weather is good, a mountain summit is the place mountaineers concoct schemes for next weekend, next month. The euphoria leads to overconfidence; eventually, the bragging is converted to commitment. For every summit achieved, a climber often adds another peak to the "must do" list. Some of us, very tentatively, added Waddington.

But I was still obsessed with getting down that narrow, exposed section. I carefully climbed down, finding that the great void bothered me less than while ascending. With so many inexperienced climbers in one large group, I could not afford to lose concentration. Finally, all were down on the ledge. It was only one rope length along the ridge to where climbers could stand on easy ground. I let Bob down and we anchored the rope as a handline for our students over the lower section. When all were down, I cast loose the upper end, assuming I could simply descend the rocks to where Bob was coiling my link to safety.

Facing down the ridge, lacking the psychological security of the rope, I could not ignore the exposure on either side. But I was embarrassed to show my fear to climbers junior to me. Despite the fact that they probably felt the exposure more acutely, I did not want them to think of their leader was afraid. More important was my need to maintain my own confidence, not to admit or give in to my own vulnerability. I finally crab-crawled on my backside, then turned face-inward for the last thirty metres, grasping with white knuckles into every surface crack. I never threw down my end of the rope again.

Along the bumps, then down from the col to the cars, many lessons suggested themselves. I had been quite justified in using a rope because of the beginners in our party, while "Harry" did the route solo and unprotected. But my reaction had little to do with reality, more to do with appearances. Intimidated by the confidence of our visiting sailor-mountaineer, I was unconsciously looking for a way to redeem myself in my own eyes, if not those of the class members. I was there to teach safe mountain practice; careless posturing did not accomplish that objective. The lesson was clear and I was lucky to learn it without consequence. It was my ego that threw down the rope that others had needed. Ego arises in many different guises, especially in the mountains.

A year or so later we discovered the "Judges' Route" on the forested west side. The rumour is that Rafe Hutchinson, a lawyer and avid climber, decided to accept an appointment as a judge while on this climb, and perhaps took some of his legal compatriots up the route.

Fewer people do the north ridge now; the "Judges' Route" is so direct. It's too easy to drive up the loggers' switchbacks, follow the trail through the timber, kick a few steps if the upper snow fields are icy; on most days you can leave the rope at home.

--oo--

While on Vancouver Island we are blessed with accessible and challenging mountains, the historical origin for climbing in Canada was in the Rockies. In 1886 the Canadian Pacific Railway had punched its rails through the Rockies past Banff and Lake Louise, then the Selkirk Mountains at Roger's Pass. A flurry of first ascents by foreign climbers ensued, showing that this would be a valuable activity for the CPR "Glacier House" hotel at Roger's Pass. But on the 1896 attempt to climb Mount Lefroy near Lake Louise, Philip Abbot, a prominent, young, American climber, fell to his death from near the summit. Concerned that climbing accidents would hinder their developing tourism, they hired European guides to work from their resorts in the Rockies and the Selkirks.

In 1906 the Alpine Club of Canada (ACC) was started from a diverse group of climbers headed by Arthur O. Wheeler. This "grand old man of the mountains", as surveyor of the Alberta-British Columbia border along the continental divide, knew the beauty and power of mountains, foresaw a future for climbing in North America. Centred in Banff, the Alpine Club built their clubhouse on the road to the hot springs on Sulphur Mountain. It became the centre of national mountaineering for Canada.

I had known of the club's reputation, but I wanted to know if it was as exclusive as I had always assumed, or accessible, as the brochures now proclaimed. I had joined the minuscule section of the club on Vancouver Island and rapidly assumed the secretary-treasurer role of a group of fewer that twenty members. It was, in effect, a private group of semi-active, elderly ex-climbers. But I wanted to know about the *main* club, its programs, the people and, above all, the valleys and ranges they traversed.

In 1972 Bob and I headed for the Rockies. Hiking into the Fryatt Creek valley south of Jasper, Alberta, we glanced over our shoulders to the stacked towers of Mount Kerkeslin, then searched ahead for the monolithic Brussel's Peak. Walking in to our first "General Mountaineering Camp" of the Alpine Club of Canada, (ACC) we scorned the club's civilized approach to what we judged to be a primitive sport. Could one be a serious mountaineer and still send their gear into camp by horse?

The trip into base camp was a long ten kilometres, especially since we insisted on carrying all our gear for the week. Horse trains passed us periodically, ferrying in the food supplies and the personal gear for all of the genteel mountaineers. When we finally dropped our packs in the soft, green upper reaches of the valley, the sight of the base camp amazed us. Canvas pyramid tents for climbers nestled into the trees. In the clearing was a huge kitchen and dining tent that could accommodate fifty persons at a time. A tall wooden flagpole was mounted beside the campfire circle; at its top Canada's red maple leaf flapped, the whole scene clashing with the deep green of western conifers.

The first day we took the climbing school, listening patiently to professional guide Hans Schwarz' threatening stories about ill-prepared climbers meeting serious accidents. He was clearly an authority, with a name to match his Swiss conservatism. But I was not ready to accept his pessimism. Amateur guides from the club assisted in the school; from them we garnered some of the lighter aspects of mountaineering. Others, like Adam Johnston on the coast, were more intent on impressing beginners, especially females, with their prowess. The fact that they had credentials superior to ours did not mollify our undisguised jealousy.

After supper, sign-up sheets for the next day's climbs were posted outside the camp manager's tent. We each picked a peak, then relaxed around the fire circle, trying to assimilate our more-than-adequate meal. Eddie Lee, a young beginner, firmly stated that the food was his only reason for coming to the camp. Public declarations seemed to be his stock in trade. We told ourselves that we were there mainly for the climbing. But when the leaders met and chose the teams, strangely, we were not on the lists for the morning start!

There was plenty of scope for day hikes and we explored the headwall of the valley and the lower slopes of

Mount Fryatt. Descending in the early afternoon, we met several decidedly elderly ladies wandering the meadow. One had just found an orchid. She led Bob through the slide alder to relocate it for us. At the campfire we met her again, patching blisters for a returning climber, explaining how to cut and fit a foam 'doughnut' around the blister to prevent boot friction. Surprised at how her athletic subject took his lesson so meekly, I asked the manager the old lady's name. "Phyllis Munday" was his answer.

Fifty years earlier she had done her own real climbing in the untracked ranges above Bute and Knight inlets on the Pacific coast. With her husband, Don, she had searched the coast ranges for their *Mystery Mountain,* spotted in 1925 from Mount Arrowsmith! For successive summers they sailed up the fjords, struggled up rain-forest choked valleys, across mammoth glaciers finally to reach the northwest peak of the massif eventually named Mount Waddington. While the summit was finally claimed by others, the discovery of the peak and its prominence (highest mountain in the Canadian provinces) and the mapping of vast unexplored icefields was their prize. By the time I knew her, Phyllis Munday was a venerated pioneer and the honorary president of the ACC. White of hair and bent of back, she was notable by her continually optimistic outlook. She loved to hear people recognize her earlier exploits (which also included an early ascent of Mount Robson), but she tried to cover any obvious pride with hurried praise of the mountains themselves.

Before dinner, Bob and I blew our only bottle of wine, treating the camp manager in the process. The next day we were both on a list for a *real* climb, a Rockies version of Mount Olympus. Assembling a party of fourteen in predawn darkness proved a challenge. Climbers straggled from various tents, forced down bowls of oatmeal, sorted their gear and fitted climbing harnesses. The assistant leader was missing; so was one of the women. Did anyone know Jenny?

Bob hollered out, "Will the real Jenny Barnett please stand up?" There was a quick rustling in one of the tents, then silence. We were down to a party of twelve.

One was Eddie, who declared (in his usual fashion) as we plodded across the snowfield to the base of the steep face. "I reserve the right to turn back at any moment!" The leader was a small man, wizened and tanned from the elements, deadly serious about rope handling and climbing procedures for his largely inexperienced crew.

"You may be many climbers, but I want to see just one set of steps up this snow face; that means some of you long-legged guys will have to shorten stride for the girls." Considering that he set the stride, there was no doubt that the steps would fit him!

Following his rules, we found the snow climbing steep but easy. We reached the rocky ridge and slogged up the broken rock to the summit. At lunch time, lolling on the flat top, we admired the distant peaks: Clemenceau icefields westward, Geikie and the Ramparts northwest, and beyond, Mount Robson. I could imagine the bewilderment of the early explorers, reaching the Continental divide not far from our summit, wondering which way to thread this sea of mountains to reach the Pacific. But there were lesser peaks nearby; most were accessible from our camp. Bob and I made our plans of imaginary climbs on impossible faces, knowing we would go only where we were told.

In those years, one still had to climb three "truly alpine" peaks to join the Alpine Club of Canada. I had expected much more from this, my first *qualifying* climb. I nearly got it. Descending the ridge, one of the climbing ropes dislodged a huge boulder. Five metres below, Eddie looked up, then froze! The leader saw it, too. He grabbed Eddie and slammed him against the cliff face just as the rock bounded over them. Eddie had nearly lost his chance to turn back.

Our leader that day was Bob Hind, considered to be one of the best amateur climbers in his heyday. Here he was, volunteering his time and skills to lead a diverse crew of beginners up a rather simple mountain. This was a pattern that I would see repeated often in the Alpine Club camps.

We took the next day off to watch Hind and Hans Schwarz climb Brussel's Peak. The main tower was vertical on all sides and their route required traverses, rappels (roping down) and more climbing. We set up our binoculars on the opposite side of the valley to trace their silhouettes. About four in the afternoon we finally spotted them on the summit. Many hours later, in the twilight of the long summer day, they returned, entering the cook-tent to a standing ovation. This was only the eighth time that the peak had been climbed!

Not all of my climbs were so easy as Mount Olympus. During the week I discovered "dinner plates," the broken (and icy) shale of Mount Lowell's west side. Again, I was surprised that a climber so proficient as John Atkinson would be leading easy climbs for the Club camps. He told me of a previous climb, of falling into a crevasse, struggling with his fear during the waiting, then, finally being rescued. He promised himself (and his family) that he would limit his risk-taking in the mountains. For a young, ambitious climber, this was a sobering concept.

Different from the instability of Lowell, Mount Parnassus was solid, but the ledges airy. The ridge we had climbed on Arrowsmith paled in comparison. I moved from one piton anchor to the next with growing confidence in the system's security. (And this time we stayed roped up until we were safely down to the snowfields.)

At the end of the week, walking out from camp down the long valley to the Banff-Jasper highway we were lighter than during our inward trip. The wine was gone. We sent some of our dunnage with the pack train. My thoughts were less concerned with the route than with the people we had met. Firstly, there were the older climbers, fifty years of age and more, who made up perhaps one-third of the camp. Some, like Bob Hind, were still doing challenging routes. Others, like Phyl Munday, were walking the meadows. But there were many others who clearly assumed that mountaineering was a lifetime activity; they were content to do average climbs, apparently for the companionship, the exercise and the scenery. Among them I had seen far less emphasis on achievement. They had reached a comfortable level in the climbing community and on a climb they were helpful, considerate, and more important, fun.

Despite our slow start, Bob and I each had climbed three summits during the camp. We would be together on camps again, usually backcountry skiing. But for the next summer camp he could not get away and I went without him.

The Glacier Lake site was located between Mount Forbes to the south and the huge Lyell Range and Glacier to the northwest. I walked in with Roger Neave. A past president of ACC, he had been to countless camps and was known to everyone we met on the trail. It was a thrill to "bathe in the reflected glory" of this well-loved veteran, even if our only point in common was that we lived on Vancouver Island. Roger was taciturn; I had time to reflect.

Jean and our two boys were in the Kootenays where she was again studying yoga at Yasodhara Ashram. We had often taken separate vacations, but I was apprehensive about the yoga she was studying, about the emphasis on becoming an "independent person." In most public courses in North America, yoga is usually physically challenging and taught in a Western, non-spiritual manner, with only a passing regard for the inner person. However, the Yasodhara approach was different. The reason for doing yoga, it seemed, was to understand one's own personality, to learn how to deal with life's crises and through the process, to grow mentally and spiritually. In my first workshop, I recognized this emphasis. The process was not Gestalt, like some rather aggressive workshop procedures I had heard about. Still it was confrontational, gently questioning many of my treasured ideas, my rather ill-defined lifetime goals.

With a good job and a growing family, I felt that things were just fine, that there was scope for growth in peripheral matters: recreation, travel, professional associations. In fact, I had not really defined my goals. I was not interested in something that threatened the status quo, that required reassessment of my basic philosophy and could upset our relationship.

Jean was involved in a search for which I felt no need; despite my Hatha Yoga practice, her quest was one that I did not understand. But our agreement was always to have some acquaintance with the other's interests. When I started climbing, Jean bought me my first iceaxe, then took the basic climbing course. She was a good climber when following, even agreeing that the sport had a certain magnetism, but she had no interest in leading routes and soon went on to other pursuits. So, I was going to have to face up to this new kind of non-physical yoga, maybe learn enough to evaluate it for myself.

The Glacier Lake camp was therapeutic. The hard work of packing up to the high camps, the focus of the climbing on Mount Forbes, the making of new friends--all made me forget the ashram. I was becoming one of the mountaineers and starting to identify with them. But, there were still many levels to reach on the peaks and in that fraternity.

On the Lyell Glacier trip one of the rope leaders reported sick on the morning of the climb. The party leader assigned me to lead what was my first Alpine Club rope. Above the high camp at the edge of the Lyell icefield, shafts of light streamed horizontally through the fog, white light through white cloud over a featureless snowfield. The place was ethereal.

We split the party into four ropes. I was allocated three climbers--each at least 50 years old--who appeared to me practically ancient. But, they all knew how to tie on, all quickly attached their *prussic* loops to the main rope. If any should fall into a crevasse these loops would form stirrups which could be moved successively up the rope to facilitate a self-rescue, assuming that the rope was stopped quickly enough when the victim fell in! But if the other ropes were nearby, this party was big enough to pull out any unfortunate--whether or not they could effect a self-rescue.

The morning cloud slowly lifted and the lead rope was able to navigate by sight rather than compass, keying on the rounded summit of Lyell II. (Five peaks ring the northwest end of the glacier, numbered from the east. The eastern three are all nearly the same height; the western two are lower but are more spectacular climbing peaks.) Nearly ten kilometres of level snow slogging separated us from our objective. By the time we started to climb to the col between the east two peaks my climbers were tiring. The sun was merciless on the glacier and we longed for the coolness of our early morning start. Despite the cumulative years of my rope's climbers, they trudged up the slope gamely, picking up the chunks of Kendall Mintcake that I left stuck in the snow for them. While they were not fast, we reached both of the summits along with the rest of the party; our rope was not the last one up either peak. Uninspiring climbs technically, they commanded incredible views and were a satisfying success. My party had developed a bond, partly from the rope connecting us; the physical effort and the summit expanse gave us all a psychological lift. We were happy to be alive and on those peaks together.

But the endless return to the high camp began to tell. Putting snow balls under our sunhats, we tried to keep our heads as cool as our feet. It was a losing battle. Before long we were alone on the glacier, trudging along as fast as my ropemates' tired old legs could take them. All the other ropes, including the party leader's rope, had long before reached the cool green of the high camp meadow when finally we slogged down the last snow slope to reach the welcome heather.

I had not taken the party leader's "desertion" with equanimity; my loss of patience must have been obvious to my charges. It irked me that these supposed expert climbers would hurry on ahead with the young and the fit, leaving a relative newcomer to deal with the flagging strength of older climbers and possible emergencies of glacier travel. When finally we reached high camp, the rest of the party was splayed on the heather, relaxing, drinking tea and, I suspected, something stronger.

Dropping the rope outside the leader's tent, I picked up my overnight gear and headed for the valley. I think that, subconsciously, I wanted him to know that it wasn't me that took so long on the glacier, that I was still game for another few kilometres. Despite the heat of the afternoon and the long effort of the climb, I didn't want to ease my anger with small talk. I also hoped he would notice!

The solo descent through the pines was pleasant in comparison to the glacier. Incredible glimpses of Mount Forbes knifing the southern horizon distracted me. The warmth of the day through the long sun hours had squeezed pungent pine resin from the forest; in contrast to the sterility of the glacier the land reeked of life. Other climbers were descending in a happier frame of mind; their humour infected me and I joined in with them.

The day's climb had been easy, but an emotional roller coaster for me: the pride I felt on being given charge of a rope, the success of our joint accomplishment on the summits, but then, my boredom and impatience on the endless return trek, plus my anger with the leader's lack of consideration detracted from the day's earlier successes.

My loss of respect for the leader perhaps was justified. Nevertheless, I had lost an opportunity to show patience, and actually, to be patient. How much better to have taken the time with my ropemates, to enjoy the end of what had been a wonderful day among the high peaks? What difference I would have experienced if I had stayed at the upper camp instead of rushing down? It was time to examine my anger and the reasons that I was going to the mountains. What were my goals, the reason for climbing? Was it the experience of the climb, the people on the rope? Or was the summit the objective? If so, for whom was I trying to get there?

Finally, I arrived at the valley bottom in time for the last setting in the dining tent, once more at peace with nature. But with my fellow mountaineers, and myself?

"The students must seek the Teacher of their own volition... they must do battle with their own doubts and undertake the discipline of their own rescue." *C. Anthony*

The Alpine Club annual camp was one thing, living on the west coast was another. You could take annual vacations in the Rockies--if you had the fee and no family to compete for time and money. Fortunately, we had another fifty weekends of the year, time to explore the local crags, and we considered the mainland mountains as acceptable material. Then, we thought of each climbing trip as an adventure, involving mainly physical exertion to reach a summit. As new mountaineers we had gathered knowledge and equipment, next was to gain experience. No one ever questioned, "Why are we doing this?" Sometimes it was aesthetics: "It's such a beautiful peak." Or "it's a classic line." At other times, a chance at fame: "the peak is still unclimbed!" But on each new outing, we learned that there were other lessons, new ways to understand the apparently simple act of climbing.

Mount Slesse appealed as a classic climb, especially the famous Buttress Route. The mountain had an aura, no matter what route you were on. Perhaps it was the fame it acquired after the 1956 accident. A passenger plane, a four engine North Star bound from Vancouver to Calgary, was returning to Vancouver airport after one engine had failed. In the turbulent winter storm it probably encountered icing conditions over the mountains, rapidly lost altitude and smashed into the south peak killing all 62 people on board. The search had gone on for months.

Elfrida Pigou was a diminutive Vancouver climber who was described by her fellow climbers as "a giant-sized pack making its way through the thickest bush, apparently unsupported." In May of 1957 she had been leading a rope, but got off the normal route into a gully to the south. It was there that she had spotted the wreckage. The peak was closed until August when a few of the bodies were found and buried and until the rumour was dispelled of secret wealth on board.

The sharp peak of Mount Slesse is visible from the Trans-Canada Highway as you drive east from Vancouver. Here the mountains form a deep coniferous horseshoe around the Fraser River valley; only the glaciated rocky peaks thrust above the green. Most are rounded, like Mount Cheam near the highway, or Mount Tomahoi just south of the U.S. border, with its long white glacier capping most of the summit ridge. But not Slesse. Its peak forms a hand reaching above the carpeted hills, its middle finger rising above the rocky knuckles in an obscene gesture to all who would approach.

Dave Tansley was familiar with these mountains. He had lived on the mainland before moving to Victoria and had started hiking in Golden Ears Park. While climbing on The Pleiades a year earlier a falling rock had knocked him unconscious, but his partner's belay held. When they finally got off the cliff, Dave was in agony with several cracked ribs but was able to walk out to the car. He showed up, encased in tape, at the office on Monday. A shy Derbyshire man, quiet to a fault in public, Dave was open and direct with his friends. His sandy hair always curled down his forehead, especially while sweating a pack up a mountain. Short, barrel-chested, with strong arms and shoulders from distance swimming, his was the ideal build for rock-climbing.

We had started climbing about the same time and were both ready to graduate from hiking, bouldering and following someone else's rope-leads, to doing our own climbs. This was only our fourth climb together; we were still getting to know each other's style--our thresholds for risk-taking. Slesse was a warm-up for a week with a guide in the Rockies.

The usual strategy on Slesse is to climb up to the shoulder in the late afternoon to avoid the heat of the day. Dave and I must have started too early or we had too much camping gear, food, and climbing "iron". All the heat of the July sun focused on the switchbacks. The grade of the trail varied from steep to very steep and our heavy loads became unbearable. The water in the canteens was soon gone and the remnant snows were still far above. Across the valley the lesser peaks began to drop away. We dumped the packs and rested, using the Border Peaks and the dark shoulder of The Pleiades as an elevation reference to check our progress.

Back on our rocky trail, we continued to struggle upward. The trees on our west-facing slope became sparse, but the waning summer sun also had lost some of its force. Finally, we dropped our packs at a flat shoulder in full view of the upthrust finger of Slesse. To its right a small glacier sloped off to the south; to the left, the west face dominated. We found a ribbon of water coming off this face. As we cooked, rehydrating on endless mugs of soup and tea, we slowly recovered from the effort of the switchbacks. In the day's last shafts of sunlight, Dave's attention was drawn to the vertical face above us and to the route descriptions copied from Culbert's guidebook, *Coastal Ranges of British Columbia.*

In the cold first breath of morning we set off from camp, loaded with more carabiners, slings and pitons than seasoned climbers would have carried. We were still testing our systems, still listening for the ring of a piton when driven into a crack, still learning which anchors would be bomb-proof if a fall occurred, and which were only psychological belays.

We crossed the sloping shoulder to the top of the snowfield and roped up for the main route on the west face. Two other climbers were on the ridge above, heading for the other route, a horizontal ledge system that connected higher up into our gully. We hoped that we could beat them to the junction. Dave led off, handling the sloping slab easily, while I paid out rope. This was safe ground, but some protection was in order, especially near the end of his rope-length lead. Halfway up he found a piton and red nylon tape-loop left by some former climber.

"This is a strange way to leave a piton," Dave called. "The tape has been threaded through the piton head and tied off!" He clipped a carabiner into the piton, glanced down at me before climbing onward. "What is that yellow stuff in the crevasse below you? Looks like a climbing rope."

I leaned outward from my anchor point, but constrained by the sling holding me to my own piton, I could see nothing. "You'd better come down and we'll have a look."

What might be tied to a climbing rope below such a popular route? Dave backed down, using his snap-link as a 'pulley' hanging on the piton. On the way he picked up a hammer lying on a small ledge. "This isn't a climber's hammer; it's a bloody claw hammer with a hole drilled in the handle for the sling!"

Just below the pitch we found a rope, uncoiled and snaking irregularly in the bergschrund where the snow pack had melted away from the rock. It was totally intact. And even better, there were no bodies tied to it. The outside woven shell (the "kernmantel") was perfect. While you can't know the history of a rope from its appearance, (how many falls it has taken, how much exposure to sun and wet) it seemed almost new.

Some rather inexperienced and ill-equipped climbers

must have tried this route for their first climb. I could just see them starting this section, (rather intimidating for a beginner), hammering in a piton, then trying to figure out how to make a runner sling to accommodate the climbing rope as it snaked upward. It was obvious that the leader had threaded the piece of nylon webbing through the loop on the carabiner, then tied it into a sling. The more normal way would have been to use a carabiner on each end of the sling. That would allow the rope to run freely away from the rock, making it easier for his climbing partner to unclip the sling, perhaps even leaving the piton for the descent.

Remembering our step by step progression from our climbing course to Arrowsmith to Slesse, I was feeling rather smug. I quoted J. M. Thorington to Dave. "Nothing is impossible or impassable if you have enough nails!"

Beginners tend to use more pitons or other anchor points because they are dealing with feelings of vertigo. Experienced mountaineers have learned to control their emotions. It was another "idea in the mind" I had been hearing about at the ashram. Apparently, a true yogi can control his imagination and exterior inputs to his mind so that he can act independently of those ideas. Usually applied to ideas of eating, sex, loyalty, etc., I was now thinking my way out of acrophobia. Excessive use of pitons was another crutch to support inexperience.

The ethic of the day was to use as few pitons as were necessary for reasonable safety--and to speed up the climb. Of course, during the climbing decades before, climbers had disparaged even the use of pitons, contending that they made the climbing more secure and allowed the lead climber to accept a higher level of risk. Later, we began to see a variety of "protection devices." Today's spring-loaded cam-type anchors were still unavailable.

We turned back to our own effort. Dave led back up, past the old piton, up the slab to a belay ledge. He found two other anchors, but we decided to set our own--ones that we could rely on. After the first rope-pitch, we found no other unusual signs. But it was hard to lose the picture of our predecessors; had these novice climbers relied too much on pitons and not developed skill and confidence first? Or were they in some accident, hit by random rockfall, or just not aware of how the exposure would affect them? Probably, they were in over their heads. It must have been traumatic, for them to abandon their equipment, especially an expensive nylon rope. I hoped that we were ready; that Slesse was not too much for us.

Through the early morning we alternated leads. While one climbed the other protected his progress, gradually getting used to the climbing speed by the rate of rope pay-out, sensing the ease or difficulty of the climbing simply by the way the rope snaked out above. Sitting below, "on belay", you could tell from the nervous whistling whether the holds were thin; you could tell by the number of pitons he placed how secure the leader felt. On my leads, I worked to keep focused, to concentrate only upon the safety of the moves and keeping the rope moving smoothly. Gradually, I started to feel confident, to set the anchors farther apart, to rely on my careful selection of holds for safety. This was pleasant rock-climbing to me, not an extreme angle, yet enough to require care.

With our delays in starting, the other climbing party had now cut into the gully above us. Periodically a pebble would ricochet down the walls while we hugged tight to the cliff. We munched our sandwiches sitting under an overhang, while pebbles and some larger rocks buzzed down, overgrown bumble bees threatening with their deadly sting. When the clatter fell silent we assumed the others had regained their ledges, out of the gully. Dave peeped out, listened and shouted. No answer.

Dave led the steep cliff above us, grunting and heaving up and over a near vertical section. On my turn, I kicked off a loose block which bounded from wall to wall, a sickening series of impacts, finally muzzled by snow and distance. The acrid smell of broken rock drifted up as I pried my fingers from the holds. We were now in a sloping trench full of loose rock. Holding the rubble together as we climbed it, we reached a col between the summit and a huge crumbling gendarme.

We could see the summit above on the left. Dave led around to the east, hammered in another "nail" and continued upward. When I reached the same point, I understood his precaution; beyond the summit block there was nothing, a vertical cliff dropping straight down to the forest. One more rope length got us up the steep bit. We were there!

All across the north and east the ranges blurred into the horizon. The Fraser River opened out to the west dividing the valley in two. To the north were the Golden Ears, Judge Howay's twin peaks, and beyond, Garibaldi. On our side, south of the river, the Lucky Four Range marched toward us.

Behind us, wires and sheets of aluminum swung lazily from the South Peak, the remains of the tragic plane crash. I was curious to actually see the point of impact, drawn by the horror of the crash. But the intervening ridge was jagged and rotten, unsafe even for expert climbers. We gazed at the wreckage, knowing that most of the aircraft and its unfortunate load of passengers had tumbled straight down the near vertical east face.

But from Slesse the most imposing view was westward, to Mount Baker, a 3,200 metre semi-active volcano. Higher than our peak, its broken north-facing glacier would be a perfect location to teach our snow and ice course. That would be on our list for next year. Its white pyramid thrust into the sky, another in the endless challenges of the Coast Range.

Self-satisfied at having completed this route, we prepared to rappel off the summit block into our gully for the descent. It had been a great climb for us both--difficult enough to require technique, patience, and conditioning--certainly not the route for a first climb.

Hearing voices, we peered over and found two climbers about fifty metres below, on the last pitch, just completing the difficult north east buttress! They could not have done that climb in a half-day and must have spent the night hanging in hammocks part way up the route. Just looking down that cliff made me feel nauseous! Compared to them, Dave and I were amateurs. They may not have viewed us in this way. But their presence put into context my earlier criticism about the owner of the abandoned yellow rope. If our assumptions were correct, that had been a novice climber who overreached on an early outing. The presence of these experts, methodically moving up the buttress toward us, was intimidating. We didn't wait around for them.

Faced with these more adventurous souls, I realized that we are all on a learning curve. We can all advance our capability by instruction, equipment and experience, but in the end there is risk, most of it "subjective", that is, risk of danger from our own actions. ("Objective" hazards are from rockfall, weather, avalanches.) A successful climber is one who becomes expert in mountain craft, then chooses climbs of appropriate difficulty to suit that ability and an internal desire for risk-taking, for adventure. Mount Arrowsmith once formed that threshold for me; Slesse would have been much more difficult without those first routes.

While climbs are not usually chosen in a conscious, rational way, a mountaineer can eventually find his own rank among others in the sport. Some reach a limit of risk beyond which they are not willing to go. Others, often leading-edge climbers, never find that boundary.

Doug Scott, a leading Himalayan climber from Britain, showed his slides for our local ACC section. As we perused the yoga and philosophy titles in our growing home library, he was fighting with the same question: "What is next? Do I back off or find a mountain or new route that has a bigger challenge?" He had just returned from an ascent of The Ogre, a very steep face in Pakistan's Karakorum Range, where he had broken both legs on the descent and been forced to crawl back to camp thus handicapped. For a climber like Scott, known for his examination of the spiritual side of mountaineering, it was not a question of competition among climbers or of his public reputation, rather a question for his searching soul.

For me, it was much less of a decision, but I was also struggling to find a balance between adventure and comfort, an acceptable level of anxiety. The spiritual rewards, the intrinsic value of mountaineering had not yet become dominant for me.

Gazing past the giant Mount Baker I noticed the vague outlines in the distance of Glacier Peak, and farther south, white peaks that could have been Mounts Rainier, Adams, or even Mount Hood, a marching row of volcanoes approximating the boundary of the North American Plate, a tectonic collision where it grinds against the northward bound Pacific Plate. While I saw those mountains, I was also unknowingly looking south along the approximate line of the Pacific Crest Trail, a route that would eventually lead me on a long, solo, introspective trek.

Quickly, we set our rappel anchor, a sling around a rock projection, and slid down the rope to the col, pulling the rope through the sling to recover it. Dave paused to organize the rope before the careful descent down the gully.

I led off, down the gully to the bergschrund where the yellow rope and the claw hammer were cached, down the endless switchbacks to where several bottles of Guiness waited, cooling in Slesse Creek.

--oo—

When Dave and I planned our trip to the Rockies, we discussed at length whether we should employ a guide. Dave would have preferred that we plan and lead our own climbs as we had on Mount Slesse. Our success on that route, while not difficult by alpine standards, had been a confidence builder. Among our group there was a popular view that a competent climber should not need a guide, that if you couldn't do the route without help, you should leave it alone. It was an elitist view.

With only two weeks of holidays and pressure on that time from families, we didn't want to waste a day looking for a route that was perfectly obvious to a guide. And we had some doubts about our readiness for Mounts Louis, Victoria and Edith Cavell, possibly even Sir Donald or Robson. Our chances were better with the help of a local expert. Ours was an ambitious list.

I had met Don Vockeroth at Glacier Lake in the Rockies, one of the few professional guides at my second Alpine Club camp. During the first week he taught a snow and ice workshop, mostly to rank beginners. About ten members of our class slogged along behind Don's faded red pack, trying to match strides with this tall and gangly mountaineer. After two hours up the marginal moraine we reached the first major snow slopes. There on the edge of the glacier we started to practise ice axe arrests used to halt a slide on steep snow.

"Gil, you go up to that overhanging cornice," Don said, "then, fall backwards off the lip and do a self-arrest before you get to those rocks below the snow!"

Was this the classic "left-handed monkey wrench" of the mountains? I couldn't tell whether he was serious. Was this Don's sense of humour? Had I been sounding-off too much about West Coast climbs during the hike up? I was about to decline his offer when one of the real novices, a woman of about 50, chose exactly that moment to lose her balance, fall over and slide down the snow. She made no attempt whatever to stop herself, tumbling and sliding on her back so she had no grip on the snow, bouncing finally head-first into the rocks.

Fearing the worst, we raced down to her, being careful not to lose control ourselves. She was splayed among the boulders, dishevelled and completely still. There was a trickle of blood matting her hair. She groaned as Don gently lifted her out of the snow, propped her up in a patch of dry gravel. She was coming around, starting to feel the pain. He checked her eyes for pupil dilation, found no evidence of concussion, so he patched-up the superficial cut on her head. We gathered up her pack and spread out Don's emergency sleeping bag to cover her. Don gave her a pain-killer and calmly settled her down to watch the rest of the practice. What a way to start a climbing school!

Whatever the situation Don seemed totally at ease in the mountains. He knew the techniques he was teaching, yet was not so threatening in his approach as most of the guide/instructors I had met. Living in Rossland, B.C., where he ran a ski shop in the winter, Don was one of the few Canadian-born members in the Association of Canadian Mountain Guides. Most of the others were Europeans, trained in the Swiss, Austrian or French Alps. Don gained almost all of his climbing background in the Rockies. It was rumoured that he had climbed every peak along the highway between Banff and Jasper.

During the next four hours the class members

learned what to do if such a fall happened to us, or to one in our party. We had practised self-arrests on Mount Arrowsmith but this was steeper and there were patches of ice to compound the danger. But there were no further incidents. By the end of the session we all felt more confident on the steep snow.

While the other students descended to the camp I stayed behind to assist. Don helped his casualty onto her feet, fashioned a sling of nylon webbing around her torso, tied-in a "handle" on her back. Then, for four long hours we descended. The woman could walk but she was extremely unsteady and naturally "psyched-out". Don kept a firm grip on the back of her harness, walked and talked her down the trail, while he trod the irregular margin. Along the top of the lateral moraine there was no room to walk beside her; the path was only a foot wide. I led and she held onto my pack; Don provided the anchor in the rear. Finally, on the meadow she relaxed and we arrived in camp, tired but happy. She left camp the next morning by horse.

Don infected others with his natural good humour; even in times of stress his smile said, "We'll soon be done with this, then we can stop for a swim in that tarn on the way down." Indeed, on one descent later in the week he stripped and dove into a freezing pond just below the snow line. Some of the females in the group were slightly embarrassed and no one followed suit. He was a guy who acted on his own impulses, yet he was universally liked.

I telephoned him about the plans Dave and I had made. Don agreed to try for three or four peaks in a ten day period. So we booked our holidays. We would split the costs of food, gas and the guide fees, sleeping in the van while en route, in tents or mountain huts while climbing.

We would start with Mount Louis. This spectacular limestone monolith is known primarily by mountaineers, tucked in behind the Mount Norquay ski hill north of Banff. Years earlier I had been skiing alone around Norquay when Louis' grey upthrust slabs sprang unexpectedly above the larch forest, totally distracting me from my ski touring. Despite that extremely cold winter morning, I had spent an hour mapping imaginary routes, even though I had yet to set foot on any serious climb. Louis was that kind of mountain.

I was happy to be back there, now knowing a little about climbing, now having a steady partner like Dave. So, on the first day of our Rockies pilgrimage we hiked up between Norquay and Edith, at a pace far too leisurely for my liking. According to the guidebook this was a long climb. My mentors had all taught me to start early, leaving hours of daylight for unscheduled problems. The weather was good and Don was in no hurry. Since he was the guide we adapted to his schedule. I kept my opinion to myself.

At the ashram they called it "suspending judgement". The teacher was always right, an attitude that I found foreign to my western upbringing, where we don't wait to question authority. I thought about the way a yoga student relates to his or her guru. The student, or aspirant, is to obey and in obedience find truth. Many times, the guru's actions or words bring the follower anger or frustration from trying to understand with limited information just what lesson is being imparted. Teachers of this kind of yoga usually do not explain; they want you to discover. Under these circumstances it is essential to suspend judgement, to avoid jumping to conclusions that hurt someone or cause the ego to become entrenched in a fixed position, a position which denies further learning.

We broke out of the trees where an avalanche chute had cleared the forest. Louis dominated the scene. Viewed head-on, the south face appears as a series of vertical ribs. From here we could not believe that it actually laid back; it really appeared to be vertical. I wondered if this was what I really wanted to do. Dave was quiet. The mountain's vertical mass was of no concern to Don. It was to me. He explained the general way we would approach, how we would get across to the ribs, what our alternatives were for descent. This was a mountain where route-finding would be critical. I consoled myself with the fact that Don had been up there many times before.

We started on the east flank, proceeding up easy slabs, roped but moving together. Don led, with only about three metres between each of us; everyone had to move at the same speed. After one or two short pitches (which Don assured us were just as difficult as anything on the upper mountain) the line traversed a ledge system, up and sometimes down, slanting left around the face to the vertical ribs on the south. Here the exposure really started to register.

The rock was no steeper than I had climbed before. In fact the rough limestone texture seemed to cling to fingers and boots. Technically, it may be true that a fall of fifteen metres is as bad as one of 300 metres, but my thinking was no longer technical. There was just too much air beneath my feet. This was a time to concentrate, to deal only with the mountain in front of me, to ignore the void below.

Don led straight up the ribs, moving smoothly and deliberately, while I belayed from the ledge. When he had run-out most of the 50 metre rope, he hammered in a piton and called me to climb. My nerves were jumping and my muscles suddenly seemed rigid. My natural climbing movements were restricted by fear of slipping; I grasped the holds far tighter than was necessary. But, I could see what I was doing, and paused to think my way through. It was then clear to me, I had done this before, the holds were good and an expert controlled the rope. I began to enjoy the movement, the mind-clearing flow that came from having a singular task at hand. Finally, there was only one "idea in my mind."

Consciously, everything focused upon the next move, on maintaining contact with the rock, on moving only one hand or one boot at a time. Yet the dominant sense was a peripheral awareness of space, nothing but space. I reached the belay, clipped the piton into the back of my harness and called Dave to climb.

Facing outward but anchored behind, I snapped a photo of Dave starting, but could not get him without including the toes of my boots. Level ground, far below, was strangely out of focus. When Dave arrived, he grinned nervously but said nothing. He was often silent, offering no opinion on the weather or other obvious factors over which we had no control (such as the extreme exposure below us); when Dave spoke it was usually worth listening. Climbing third, he was lacking the direct connection to our guide that I enjoyed as the second. Later, he felt that this contributed to his nervousness throughout that day. During the climb he never let it show.

Don readied his hardware and slings for the next pitch. We proceeded, one rope-length after another, up the ribs to the base of the final chimney, generally considered the "crux" of the climb. There, a choice had to be made, whether to climb inside the chimney where holds are scarce but the cliff below is less obvious, or to scale the rock to the right, where the holds are better but the exposure is incredible.

Don chose the outside, the right hand route, and led off. Ten metres ran out. That meant a twenty metre fall before the strain would hit me if he came off. Finally, he paused to drive in a piton, fix a snap-link in the eye, and run the climbing rope through it. If he should fall now it would be only double the distance down to his piton--

assuming the piton held! I could not see that anchor because of the bulge in the cliff face, but I paid out the rope steadily. When I had only two metres left, I called it out and Don halted. In a few minutes he shouted down, "Climb!"

As I carefully eased out onto the slab, I was immediately aware of the 800 metre cliff below me, nothing between my feet and the apron we had scaled two hours earlier. I could not believe that he had climbed out here, and then even higher, before he had set any anchor! But then, he was the guide.

I edged slowly up the face, choosing holds carefully for my boots, reaching ahead for handholds that would be in the right place for my next step upward. Consciously, I kept my fingers crimped tight to my palms so that my grip would be stronger if my feet came off. As I came up to Don's carabiner, I clipped the rope out to pass it, then ran the trailing part back in, so that it would guide Dave's rope. Just above the anchor the holds were so thin that I could hardly find them. There were only two little cracks, maybe a finger width wide--wide enough to play on while boulder-climbing down at the beach, but not to rely on, suspended hundreds of metres above nothing. My calf muscles started to vibrate; I had to move, and quickly!

"Tension!" I shouted, and reached for a small knob of rock above me. Don snaked the rope upward, but I didn't wait for it to catch up. I grabbed the next hold, and the next, and soon reached his belay point.

We were perched right on the round-out at the top of the cliff. When I clipped in, I could begin to ignore the exposure. Don belayed Dave for that pitch.

To the south I saw the geological wave in the strata; syncline--antisyncline--syncline marched off to the horizon, the broken and weathered peaks grey and black through the melting snows of summer. Assiniboine, Canada's

“Matterhorn”, interrupted the pattern to the south, projecting above intervening ranges. To the west was the Sleeping Beauty Range near Lake Louise, luminous white in the sun, dominated by the mass of Mount Temple. Despite the rough hewn topography the horizon showed the earth's curvature. Our precarious perch further emphasized our minuscule size in the natural world.

Dave arrived at the top of the crux pitch. While I had been peak-gazing he had mastered the toughest part of the mountain. In comparison, the remaining scramble to the summit was an easy walk. We shot pictures all around, including one of the cross on the summit, Don behind with the sun at his back, a halo above his hardhat.

While we ate, Don told stories about previous climbs on Mount Louis, of times when the weather was less inviting. The peak is a magnet for storms, especially electrical displays. On one trip he had been hit by a storm while belaying his friends down the west face. Usually, climbers try to get rid of their iron equipment during these storms, because if the lightning doesn’t kill you, it can cause extreme muscle convulsions, making it difficult to hold on. Several times he had received huge charges of static electricity, but they all survived; when the convulsions hit him all the climbers on the rope had been held because of his piton anchored to the rock.

Don stuffed his gear in his pack and got up to go. “Down-climb the route we climbed,” he asked, “or rappel off the west side?” Dave, who had been climbing third on the rope, was feeling uncomfortable about the route we had just finished. I did not relish retracing the crux pitch, even with a top rope. On the other hand we both enjoyed rappelling, sliding down a doubled rope, controlling the speed by the friction of the rope around your shoulder and back, paying out as fast or as slow as you wanted using your lower hand.

A rappel is very committing. You have to believe in your anchor, your equipment and yourself. If any one of these fails, you will have a long, and probably fatal, fall. It is this requirement of total self-reliance that makes it a so frightening, especially backing out over the edge. As with so many real trials we face, the first step is the most difficult.

Our first rappel was not vertical; it was on a side-sloping slab that kept pulling you towards the overhang on the right side. Dave went first. When he was down I rappelled next, using a "dulfersitz", a nylon webbing sling I could sit in. Using a carabiner, I could clip it into the rope for the descent. Don was not happy. He preferred the classic rappel system in which only the rope is used.

"One thing less to go wrong, eh?"

But when he realized I was wearing blue jeans, knowing that the rope would burn if I slid directly down the rope, he relented. We completed that descent with only one close call when a loose rock bounded down, narrowly missing the rope. Then some tricky route-finding; even Don was uncertain which of the bluffs should be next, till he found the tell-tale piton anchor above a vertical pitch. The next three rappels were short and well anchored. We were starting to relax. There was only one left; it would get us down to the scree ridge and provide an easy route to the valley.

But what a drop! Don tied both ropes together--50 metres hanging free--but still it hung a couple of metres short of the ridge.

"When you get there, just jump," was his solution.

I went first. Don had found three existing pitons, anchors left by other climbers, and connected them all together with a new sling. Getting over the lip of the ledge was awkward. The cast off point was very confined; I had to pull the rope up over my shoulder, clip it into the carabiner on my dulfersitz, then back outward, squeezing between walls only two feet apart. The anchor was at my feet. Until I got below the anchor the whole system was be very unstable. Kneeling down, I shifted my weight from my knees to the rope, arranging the sling so that it did not press against any jagged rock surface.

I let the rope inch out, sliding through my right hand. It moved up my back, over my left shoulder and through the dulfersitz carabiner. I started to feel in control. The cliff was slightly overhanging so that soon I was clear of the rock on a free-hanging rope. Steadily descending, avoiding any sudden jerk on the anchor, I moved suspended between earth and sky.

Then the rappel stuck! I couldn't go down any further. The hood of my anorak had been pulled around my shoulder by friction and had jammed into the carabiner. The rope had firmly anchored it into the hole the rope slid through. It was going nowhere!

From many metres above me I heard Don's voice. "Have you got a knife? You'll have to cut the hood off."

"My new anorak? You're kidding! Besides, the knife is in my pack and I only have one free hand."

There was a small ledge about three metres to the right where the rock didn't overhang. I began pumping, like on a playground swing, and soon I was able to catch the ledge, take some of my weight off and pull out the hood.

For the remainder of the rappel I was very careful to keep my hood away from the rope. At the bottom I lowered myself as far as I could and dropped to the scree.

Dave and Don followed, both using the classic method (avoiding my problem of clothing stuck in the carabiner.) Then, Don yanked on one part of the doubled rope as he jumped down to the ridge and we dragged it through the sling left abandoned at the top.

Back on flat Dave and I breathed easier. I just lay

back on the scree and closed my eyes, emptied all that tension out of my lungs. We were exhilarated, me especially because of the last rappel. We recounted all of the dangers of the climb and the rappel descent. For the first time since the start, ten long hours earlier, relaxed and animated conversation flowed. Even stoic Dave was bubbling!

Dumping our harnesses, we coiled the ropes and packed up for the hike out. The route was straight forward--down 400 metres of steep scree, then east between Edith and Louis till we hit the main trail. We agreed to meet at Rosemary's Restaurant in Banff for supper. We had been climbing since early morning; Dave and I wanted to wander downward, to slowly release the tensions of the day, to soak up the surroundings and the experience.

Don was now strangely full of energy. He charged off ahead to visit with his friends in town. His day was far from over.

--oo—

Neither Dave or I had wanted to lead the rope on Mount Louis. Its apparent verticality and size clearly intimidated us both. Still, we wanted to progress, to get beyond the easy peaks on Vancouver Island, to start to push our rather minuscule envelope. We were happy to have an expert to route-find and to do the exposed climbing on Mount Louis, but we had to learn from the guide, then emulate him.

For some time, I had thought in terms of a guide being somewhat like a yoga guru, even though the mountain guide isn't necessarily going to get inside your head like a guru might! Of course, Dave was not into the philosophies either of gurus or guides! But even without the benefit of yoga, he wanted someone who would let us lead parts of the climbs. We had both heard horror stories of guides whose only concern was to get the party to the top and back safely, with little regard for the quality of the experience. But I had seen Don Vockeroth in action; I knew his approach was different. Fortunately, Dave was happy to accept my opinion. After Mount Louis we drove to Lake Louise. We had done a major rock route; now for a snow climb. We chose Mount Victoria, the broad triangular snow peak above the lake, perhaps the most photographed mountain in Canada.

We had arranged to meet him at ten in the morning at the "Plain of the Six Glaciers", a teahouse at the upper end of the lake. We had to go up to the Abbot Pass hut on the col between Mounts Victoria and Lefroy where the climb would begin. The route to the hut followed a deep, narrow trench below the glacier that hung from Victoria. Chunks often broke off, endangering anyone below, so it was best to go through early and quickly, avoiding the warm afternoon when the summer sun would weaken the poised snow face. The route was variously called the "deathtrap" or, as we preferred, the "mousetrap."

Dave and I were at the meeting place by the appointed time. Through the morning we lay around on the meadow, stiffening up from the unaccustomed effort the previous day. By 3 o'clock in the afternoon, our patience was wearing thin. It really didn't matter when we got up to the hut as long as it was in time for the next day's climb. And as long as the snow above was still stable... It gave me another opportunity to surrender to what I took as the caprice of our guide.

Finally, about 6 pm, Don loped up the trail carrying in his hand two huge cream-puffs from Doc's bakery in Banff, presumably as a peace offering. But no apology. He was warmed up and rolling. He seemed to flow up the trail, despite the huge rucksack he carried. While he was probably no older than I, nudging his forties, his tall and slender frame hinted at the endurance of a seasoned mountaineer. His light brown hair was in customary disarray, curls bobbing down his cheeks, stuck at the temples by a trickle of sweat. His eyes were sky blue and laughing.

We had been there eight lethargic hours and found it difficult to gear-up to Don's speed. But since this was probably the worst possible part of the day to traverse under those overhanging cliffs we trotted up to the hut in two hours.

Poised at 2922 metres on the pass between Mounts Lefroy and Victoria, the hut had endured winter storms and the passage of summer climbers since 1922. With stone walls, small windows and wooden plank beds, it was a romantic first mountain hut for Dave and me. We drank endless cups of tea (with jam left by some previous climber) and cooked our curried beans. Don traded stories with another party who had come up from the Yoho valley on the other side of the pass. As we absorbed the discussion of routes and made new friends we started to appreciate the value of huts as meeting places.

Despite the fresh snow on the lower rocks we were up to the ridge on Victoria to greet the morning sun rising over Lefroy. Along the crest of the great glacier there were no real technical difficulties--only care and attention was needed to keep the rope stretched out between us, to stay close to the cornice, yet not walk on it. And we kept our crampons tight-strapped to our boots and clear of soft snow. Whenever they collected too much in the cleats, it was like standing on a pair of platform shoes with Teflon soles. Some years before, a Japanese party had slipped down that magnificent snowfield, over the cliff into the "mousetrap." Experts presumed that they had let the snow pack into their crampons, rendering them useless on the sun-softened surface of the glacier.

The summit of Victoria, at 3465 metres, is the focus of the Sleeping Beauty Range. From so high, we could command a longer view than from Mount Louis. Lake Louise itself was an insignificant puddle and the Chateau Lake Louise, a dollhouse. In the valleys on either side of the range, man's incursions seemed barely visible. The ski development on Whitehorn Mountain, the roads into Lakes O'Hara and Louise, all were mere threads through the forests.

The climb itself was not so demanding as on Louis, or as it would be on our next climb. We descended from the summit, retracing our route to a notch in the ridge, then with Dave leading, we dropped through the gap westward and descended that glacier past Mount Huber toward Lake O'Hara. We paused at the toe of the snowfield above a steep rock cliff. As we snacked on sardines and crackers a light breeze blew from Huber and Victoria at our backs; a plume of blown snow drifted horizontally from our summit, its whole ridge now fused into a milky blue sky.

Don unclipped his carabiner from the rope. "Time to drop the rope," he said as he started to coil it for his pack.

"But without it, which way do we get down?" Dave asked, incredulous.

"Straight down this rock to the Wiwaxy Saddle, over there on the left."

"You're kidding," I couldn't believe him. "That's easily as steep as parts of the route on Louis!"

"Believe me," said Don. "Just follow the trail of little stone men. We'll be down the cliff in twenty minutes."

And we were. It was not at all like Mount Louis, but rather a series of staircases winding left and then right. There was no lack of security there. Don had established his right to be our guide. He knew the routes, his technique always favoured safe climbing without instilling fear at every step. It is reasonable to expect these qualities in an alpine guide.

In yoga, I had heard the guide described in three forms: the mystical guide, the guru, and finally, self-knowledge or the "guru within." The first is a spiritual presence, sometimes seen in a physical form while under deep meditation or in the stress of a crisis, often near death. Once, at the ashram, I had felt it. My own spirit seemed to leave my body and, attached by a vague lifeline, floated above me in the room. I seemed to be in control of the separation, not wanting to end it. Others in the room started to move about, finishing their meditation. Finally, I came back, slowly emerging into full consciousness. I was left with a feeling of confidence and peace, an understanding that there were levels of existence yet to experience.

Native people describe this spirit as an animal form, and it gives them guidance for major decisions in life, or leads their spirit from one level to another after death. In yoga instruction, the appearance of such guides is considered a "gift" from another level of consciousness to be received with gratitude. We were told it was not an adventure to be sought after. In fact, we had many exercises to help us define our purpose, our ideal in life. These, and workshops wherein we worked on correcting our personality problems, were intended to prepare us for such unexpected occurrences to give us awareness and openness to such new ideas and phenomena. In practical terms, such a "guide" usually might be inspirational but not instructional in the sense of solving life's questions.

Secondly, the guru I took to be the closest metaphor of the climbing guide. A yoga aspirant must be extremely selective in the choice of a guide. Once chosen, the guru is to be obeyed in all cases. The guru-aspirant relationship lasts much longer (often a lifetime) and is often a noncommercial transaction. Nevertheless, there are many similarities to the climbing guide. Once we employed Don, it is very unlikely that we would disagree with his route or some detail of achieving the objective. There may be doubts, but confidence is built by his/her reputation, or from alpine routes climbed together, in the same way as your guru might help you to understand lessons of life. In both cases, you surrender some part of your free will to reach some new plateau, physical or psychic.

The real teacher will allow the student to discover and thus to validate his or her own understanding. I found this aspect of yoga especially trying. If there was a lesson I needed to learn, whether it be the meaning of a dream, the experiences I might meet during meditation, or simply something that I needed to learn about my behaviour or attitude, I wanted someone to tell me. But the ashram followed the Buddhist way of offering only minimum guidance, frustrating as it was to me. It would be a poor alpine guide that would let the new climber discover the best knot for connecting to the rope, simply by trial and error! On the other hand, the teaching of the spiritual aspects of mountaineering must allow for self-discovery.

In yoga, the final phase of learning is one in which a practising yogi (or yogini) becomes independent of other earthly guides and listens only to his own counsel. This self-knowledge is sometimes called the "guru within"; it can supplement or eventually replace the teacher.

The mystical guide, or spiritual presence can occur unexpectedly or during some epiphany in one's life. On the other hand, the "guru within" is developed over years of study, contemplation, and increasing awareness. The student (or by this time, the practising yogi) is getting direction, inspiration or intuition from some source, from spiritual beliefs or from experience. If you believe in a separate, all-knowing presence, you could say that the inspiration or direction comes from God. For me, I accept the idea of a higher being, but still a part of me, one that I have to learn to access. Naturally, these definitions of stages are rather arbitrary. In fact, the lines between the three arbitrary definitions blur. And this is also true in the mountains. Neither Dave nor I had felt cheated by Don leading on the first two of our mountains. Indeed, we were delighted with his knowledge of the Rockies, his experience, his attitude. It seemed that everyone from Banff to Jasper knew Don and we were often included in the events of his social life. So we were content to ignore unimportant matters. Punctuality was not a big deal; we were on holidays. Down at the Lodge at Lake O'Hara his reputation got us in for tea and civilized snacks despite our rugged clothes and several days growth of stubble. In favour of Lodge ambience, we almost missed the bus back to our van at Lake Louise!

We discussed our next climb. We were working our way north, with Mount Robson as a possible dream objective at the end. "We'll meet at the Columbia Icefields parking lot tomorrow at ten in the morning." Don stated. "If you want to try Robson, best you do the Skyladder on Andromeda first. The top 400 metres of Robson is the same, but Andromeda is in a friendlier environment."

The Skyladder was impressive only to climbers. Of the thousands of Icefield tourists driving by on the highway or riding the glacier in snowmobile buses, few would ask about that little ice slope above the glacier on the left. Dwarfed by Mount Athabaska, the Snow Dome and Andromeda itself, it wouldn't rank a mention in a tourist brochure.

We had only to walk an hour beyond the snowmobile terminus. Some of these lower ice slopes were covered with moraine gravel frozen into the surface, making walking difficult without crampons. Finally, we put them on; it was the lesser evil. As we crossed on the level glacier, the crampons balled-up with sticky soft snow. The face above appeared vertical. If the snow up there was soft like this, it would never stay on such a slope, and neither would we. The ice slope started from the bergschrund, where the moving glacier (below) separated from the fixed ice frozen to the slope. It was a continuous ramp right up to the round-off near the summit. We arranged our ropes and checked our gear at the foot of the slope. Don found a snow bridge on the right and we moved into an inclined world.

Most climbers, beginners and even experienced alpinists, overrate the steepness of their special routes. This one was very intimidating to Dave and me, whose biggest snow climb to that time had been the Roman Wall on Mount Baker, about 35 degrees to the horizontal. The Skyladder was a full 50 degrees.

For the next three hours I exerted a greater concentration than ever before. All of my senses were focused on the climbing, on deliberate movement in balance. We set bomb-proof anchors where the snow was deep and firm, digging in an iceaxe across the slope in a narrow trench. As belayer, I would dig-in below, with my harness clipped to a sling around the iceaxe handle. The belayer always faces downslope in such conditions, to where the tension would come in the event of a fall. Then, Dave climbed the slope above. When the rope was nearly all out, I called, "Two metres!" Dave then prepared a similar belay, dug in and hollered for us to climb.

Don tied himself into the middle. Each of us led the full fifty metres, from last position right through to the lead. Then the other would repeat the same procedure. Don coached from the middle, but there was very little said during the entire climb. We were getting our chance!

The snow was about 10 cm deep to start, firm and well frozen to the hard ice beneath, wonderful for crampon climbing. As we climbed higher the snow petered out, leaving bare ice; only our front four crampon points were in contact. There, on the exposed ice, we used tubular ice-screws, wound down into the ice about the length of my hand. But on a slope so steep it would be extremely difficult to stop a fall, with obvious consequences for our whole rope. So, we climbed very carefully, moving one at a time. The muscles in my calves screamed at the constant stretching. The Skyladder was becoming an endless succession of ice hockey rinks, strung together end-to-end and tilted at 50 degrees.

Spindrift wafted across the ice, kicked up in our faces, but the sun held the sky, promising no change in conditions for the remainder of the climb. I was entirely on the front points of the crampons, keeping my heels as low as possible to increase the contact. I used an iceaxe held over the head with one mitt and an ice-screw in the other. One hand or one foot moved at a time--three points in contact at all times. Think, balance, move. Think, balance, move! It was pure meditation.

"Three metres to go!" Dave called from somewhere outside my world. I climbed five steps more. Then, starting an ice-screw into the surface I wound it around, spiralling it downward into the rock-hard slope of polished ice. I unclipped another screw from my belt, fed it through the loop of the anchor to get more leverage, worked it down till the cored ice squeezed out the top of the hollow tube. That would hold a lot, maybe even a fall. Clipping-in with sling and carabiner to my harness, I turned to face down that awful ramp, squatted down so that the sling was tight, then jammed all points of each crampon into the slope. "On belay!"

Don unclipped from his stance and came up, climbing easily. "O.K. Dave, you climb through again and set the next anchor. You'll need a screw; there is no snow left from here on up." Dave dug out his axe which had been the belay and prepared to climb. Just as he started up a huge black bird ghosted beneath him, far down the slope. We were climbing above the ravens.

Station upon station, rope-length upon rope-length, we continued. Only when the slope started to lay back, at the moment that we could see over the round-out to the summit beyond, did fatigue set in. And, of course, there had been the focus of fear. But it was more like an intense carefulness. I had thought of nothing but the climbing for the whole route.

On the top we unroped. Classic peaks of the Rockies were all around: Snow Dome, Athabaska, even Mount Columbia to the west. Below us the ant-like snowmobiles ferried their tourists out onto the glacier for the thrill--of what? Of standing on real, ancient, glacial ice.

The descent was anticlimactic despite a whipped cream cornice we crossed beneath, despite a long snow chute we plunge-stepped down. My sinuses were active, Dave had a migraine, sure signs of a stress-filled day. Fortunately, during the climb, nothing had bothered us.

Next morning we drove to Jasper. Don got reports from more of his friends. No one had done Mount Robson yet that year; it was definitely out-of-condition with too much snow and another weather system moving in.

We had done three peaks in four days, but we still had time before our holiday deadline. Don told us about the route on Mount Edith Cavell. We could do it on our own, easily. We hoped that we could traverse it from east to west as our last climb of the series. Perhaps now, we were ready for the "guru within" to take charge and to lead us on this mountain. We had built confidence on two very demanding routes—Louis and the Skyladder. Would we have the discipline to make decisions that the mountain and weather would dictate? We felt ready.

But, as we drove up to the lake below Edith Cavell's north face, the rain started. In the morning, more rain followed hard on our heels up the east shoulder. When it turned to snow on the steep rocks of the ridge at the start of the hard climbing we called it a week. Our Rockies adventure, like the weather, was slowly unravelling.

AWARE OF THE MOUNTAIN Self Discovery

"He who sees the inaction that is in action, and the action that is in inaction, is wise indeed." *Bhagavad Gita*

"Climbing is a living metaphor for unifying one's existence."
G.B.Schaller

Weather dictates everything you do in the mountains. Deterioration of the weather often signals the end of a climbing adventure. If you are lucky you will be able to head home or to a warm mountain hut. There are subtle changes, too, and even a warming trend can be a harbinger of trouble. In winter you expect miserable days, so when the sun finally breaks through, it is difficult to restrain yourself.

During the '75 Alpine Club ski camp on Kootenay Glacier the snow came with wind on the higher slopes, forming a consolidated slab over the soft underlay. The next morning had dawned so incredibly clear and bright that when we stepped from the cabin into the fresh fluff that had settled gently in the valley it was easy to ignore any avalanche hazard. Contouring west from the cabin towards the day's objective of Mount Geigerich, Bob and I with two others climbed steadily along the south rim of the valley.

We were using an ordinary type of downhill ski, except that our harness allowed the boot to pivot at the toe while climbing. We used "skins" strapped under our skis for traction. The original ones had been made from sealskin; ours were synthetic, with the fibres pointing toward the tails of the skis. They would slide ahead, but not backwards. When we would reach our high point, the skins went into the packs; the boot heels clamped down and we would be ready to *schuss*. In these mountains every run was virgin, waist-deep powder, effortless skiing streaming a rooster tail behind!

On the way to Geigerich, a steep gully blocked our

route. It was a thousand metres down to the valley bottom, or two hundred metres up to an uncertain ridge by-passing the gully. Neither option was very attractive. The obstacle was really a gentle concave slope, so I thought the snow crust would be mainly in compression. However, at the top of the gully there was a worrisome bulge. Nowadays, we would dig a snow pit to check the strength of the lower layers in the drift.

We decided to take a chance. As lead skier, I removed the pole loops from my wrists and unhooked my ski safety straps. Taking a deep breath, I slanted my skis downward, shooting for a point about thirty metres across.

Halfway across all hell broke loose. The whole slope suddenly was moving. Immediately submerged in sliding, twisting chunks, there was no way to ski out of it. I tried to swim, flailing about, trying to knock off my skis. I couldn't tell up from down. Both legs felt twisted and stretched, as if they were in a washing machine. Chunk after chunk broke off the bulge at the top, feeding the river of churning snow. The whole mass slid toward the lower cliff edge. I was drowning, despite my desperate backstroke.

Suddenly, it stopped. I was only a few metres short of an awful ride to the bottom of Griffin Creek valley.

I could still feel all my appendages; my face was clear so I could breathe. "That was a chance I should not have taken," now I knew!

At least the slope was stabilized. Bob led the others down through the strewn blocks to where I had freed my arms. A bit of shovelling uncovered my skis and the residual twisting from nature's "mixmaster" was relieved. The only thing missing was a ski pole. Nothing was broken; I had been extremely lucky!

On the far side of the gully we reassembled, checked over my equipment. Bob cut and fashioned a ski pole from a scrub slide-alder to replace the one buried out of sight. We continued on toward Geigerich, keeping a cautious eye on any slope we had to cross. We avoided south-facing slopes that had been loaded by the wind and now were settling in the sun's warmth. I was suspicious of every cliff or cornice. Later that afternoon we reached the glorious summit in plenty of time to enjoy the view and the long run back to the cabin. Avoiding any traverses across gullies, we found safe skiing in the creek valleys below Lemon Pass and, following the terrain eastward, schussed in perfect powder down to the cabin in the valley.

Considering how narrow my escape, I had been surprisingly calm. The nearness of death that day registered for several months in repeated, suffocating dreams. And in similar conditions on later snow climbs I was always first to insist on retreat. It was a lesson I had over-learned.

That spring, I was back in south east British Columbia, but this time across Kootenay Lake at Yasodhara Ashram. Jean had finished one summer of her course and still had to complete several of the book reviews on the mandatory list. She was into regular practice at our home in Victoria, doing Hatha yoga asanas and relaxation, taking time most days for quiet contemplation. On Sunday evenings at our home, a few friends would arrive for "satsang," group chanting and affirmations, followed by socialising. Jean found that chanting for long periods was especially helpful, clearing her mind and assisting in relaxation. Called Japa Yoga, its repetitions can be verbal (as in singing a mantra) or written many, many times. The effect is that you can eliminate worries (repetitive thinking in a "loop,") or get rid of scattered thoughts, sometimes referred to as "the monkey mind," thus making yourself ready to act or think more clearly.

I had left my job as a structural engineer, thinking that I might work on my own, specialising in some aspect of engineering or construction. Before deciding, I would take the ashram's "Teacher's Course." They call it something else now, perhaps for liability reasons; it now implies that the student has studied yoga in depth, but is not necessarily qualified to instruct in all forms of yoga. The same series of courses that Jean had taken over two summers, I would do it in four consecutive months. I wanted to learn more about her pursuit and, at the same time, give myself time to consider my future, rather than just leaping into something. This sounds logical now, but it had not been my pattern!

So, my own study began. By this time less apprehensive of the mysteries of yoga, I sweated through intensely personal workshops, writing long, introspective papers about my ideals, emotional reactions and relationships. Haltingly, I became aware of the fact that I was not perfect! It is hard to see change in yourself, even in retrospect, but I perceived two faults that I wanted to change. I was far too dependent upon the good opinion of other people, reacting to their goals for me, seeking their praise. Secondly, I had not been very clear about expressing my feelings, good or bad, partly because I had seen a lot of negative diatribes from my father as a boy. Unconsciously, I controlled my own negative explosions, but substituted for them in other ways. I didn't get rid of those feelings, I just transferred them to others or to other situations. I nagged my family a lot!

Most of my work was about Jean and me, about the meaning of responsibility, dependency, and love. I sent letters to Jean in Victoria. She answered about her own work at home. And the rest of my "stuff" was about Dad.

Among the siblings of our family there was a clear consensus about our parents. Whenever my brothers and sisters (two of each) and I discussed family, we agreed that Mom was a saint and Dad was the opposite. There was no doubt that my mother had been an exceptional woman. Eldest child of a large Saskatchewan farm family, she had matured early, going out to teach junior grades in a local school while still in her teens. She met Dad in one of the towns where she taught--he was a handsome Alberta logger, just emigrated from Chicago, working to a secure a homestead. With two oxen he farmed his land in summer and dragged logs to market in winter. According to several of our aunts, the two started fighting immediately after they were married. But Mom realized the effect this would have on the children and her marriage; she gave in to a life of acquiescence. Yet, as children growing up in such a family, we always felt she was the leader, the stronger personality. Her code was pacifism, especially in the face of his verbal (and sometimes physical) violence. Increasingly, Dad became isolated in his own family.

In many ways, he was a product of his generation. The male was expected to be the head of the family, his wife the passive housewife and nurturer of his children. He was the disciplinarian, the enforcer of a strict, impossible set of rules for young, inventive children to follow. But he had been the youngest of his own family, with little experience of healthy family dynamics. He did not know how nor when to compromise on rules, considering infractions to be a personal affront to authority, reacting with excessive punishments.

After all of the older children grew out of the home, I was left alone, four years younger than Ken, next in age to me. I had to deal with Dad's anger as an "only child" just into my teens. At that stage in our lives, we were living a hard, physical life in the remote hinterland of Alberta's Peace River country. I did not mind the continual chores. There was little social life anyway and I could usually escape to the bush to shoot grouse or snare rabbits. But Mom had to bear the brunt of his tirades; there were times that I would have killed him, if I could have found the courage.

After I left home, this anger became somewhat muted, but I still held him in an isolated capsule. I had as little as possible to do with him. But at the ashram, through the various workshops, I came to realize that his violence was born of his own immaturity, exaggerated by the custom of the day. Many fathers were caught in the same box. I discovered that my own feelings were a carry-over from my youth, keeping *me* in a prison of hidden emotion. My nurtured hate was hurting me more than it was him.

A year earlier, my mother had died in a long-term care hospital from Parkinson's Disease. Her death followed after a period of progressive weakness culminating in her total inability to communicate. I could not know what she was experiencing or what it was she was trying so hard to tell me; I only knew that it was painful to visit her. Her death was a release for me and, hopefully, for her.

The ashram's probing workshops helped me to realize that it was time for me to let go of my resentment. It couldn't have happened at a more fortuitous time. One night after dinner someone called down to the dining hall that there was a telephone call for me. With only one public phone we seldom heard from anyone; Jean and I would exchange calls only if it was an emergency. With some trepidation I ran up to the booth and grabbed the receiver.

"Hello, Gilbert?" It was Dad. "I have been meeting an old friend from near my Rosenthal homestead. She lives in Vancouver and we have decided to get married. Will you come and represent the family?"

I was flabbergasted! I had no problem with him remarrying--even if he was over 70 and his intended, Carrie, was older still. I had no lingering loyalty to Mom, at least not related to what Dad might do. But, what really amazed me was that he would even consider asking me. I couldn't remember us having exchanged a civil word when I was a teen, and after Jean and I were married, we visited infrequently and stuck to strictly superficialities. In the end,

I decided that he called on me because I was closest; they were to be married in Vancouver.

It was a welcome break in ashram routine. For the event I drove to Vancouver and met Jean and the boys coming off the ferry. We presented ourselves at the Catholic Church off Hastings Street. It was a huge building with space for several hundred more than our small attendance of perhaps fifty. Most were nuns from the seniors' home in which Carrie had been living. (Dad probably thought he was rescuing her.) The rest were Carrie's family. There was no bride's side or groom's side. Still, I could see why he wanted some balance. Behind Dad, our little family of four trouped down to the front pew.

"You don't have to worry," Dad whispered in his throaty roar, at the decibel level common to the nearly deaf, "she's got lots of money!" A titter ran through the crowd. I hadn't been worrying.

Eventually, Carrie and Dad were asked to approach the altar on the wide and elevated stage for the ceremony in front of the priest. On Carrie's side was her niece; beside Dad I stood wondering how I had ever become my Dad's "best man."

"Do you take this woman..." intoned the priest. Dad looked at me vaguely.

"Do you take this woman?" I spoke directly into his ear. And on it went, with me relaying the instructions of the priest into the deaf ears of the principals. Perhaps priests are not allowed to shout in church.

Finally, it was over. The happy couple (and they would be, my father being very lucky with his women) would be living in Edmonton in an apartment complex for the elderly. There was an amicable reception at the apartment of Carrie's niece. Then I headed out on the highway to the Kootenays again and my family ferried to Victoria. I wouldn't see them until my course ended, another long month later.

On the long drive back I took stock of my ashram course. There had been little definition of the various aspects of yoga that we were learning. I don't think I ever saw a course outline. I had heard of Hatha and Japa yogas, but now I was learning other approaches: Bhakti yoga, the approach of love, and Karma yoga, which encourages responsible actions and helpful support of other humans, and indeed, all life. The term karma had practically entered the English language, as in "if you don't share that chocolate you will accumulate bad karma!" Really, these approaches to yoga are somewhat more complex than just "being good." There was Prana yoga, using breathing exercises, and Laya, Jnana, and Raja yogas, all different routes to self-realisation.

What did they mean to me? While the language describes hundreds of practices and philosophical explanations, I took them all to be "understanding everything" or "knowing God." I realized that there were many phenomena in the world that I could not explain, but I looked for spirituality within myself. For my own definition of God, I had to understand all aspects of myself, and realize all of my capabilities. That might not be achieved overnight!

The work went on; Hatha yoga before breakfast, specific workshops morning and afternoon, perhaps some time for independent writing before dinner, then satsang, or prayer meeting, before bed. It was a full program. Periodically, a visiting guest or Swami Radha, the leader of the ashram, would give a talk. Radha's were rambling stories about her training in India and the experience of establishing the centres in Canada, but she had a deft way of bringing a concrete point into these tales. She was an entertainer, in a sense, but one with a clear purpose, too.

And what had I gained in the process? Well, apart from reaching a belated détente with my father and becoming conversant with the range of studies Jean was working through, I slowly learned that anger can be expressed without personal malice. This allowed me to show affection, as well. Personality doesn't change overnight, but I was getting more clarity of what contributed to relationships, and what detracted.

I began to think differently about approval of others. A concrete result of this attitude became apparent in my public speaking. Most of my performances were a disaster. I expected to appear intelligent, incisive and persuasive—and failed miserably. As soon as I was on my feet, I would become self-conscious, forgetting the points I needed to make. But, as I learned to forget myself, to focus only on the material, I experienced a vast improvement.

Most apparent to me at the time, I was understanding "process," emphasising the work and play of life—the experience, not just achieving the goal. I had always been able to finish projects, but I had not appreciated the journey. Changing the focus rounded off my edges.

At the end of the four months we all returned home, there to continue our practice and evaluate our own progress. In the summer Jean and I reversed our venues. I worked in Victoria while the family was at the ashram for a summer of holidays and, of course, study for Jean. I drove up there for two weeks holiday. Jean was busy with her classes and papers. I practised Hatha yoga exercises and went swimming in the lake with the boys. There were a few days left in my August holiday. I remembered the ski pole that I had lost in the avalanche. I felt a magnetic attraction to that place, like a robber returning to the scene of his crime. So, I drove with Ross, now 11 years old, and Glen, who was 9, up to the trailhead.

Ross especially liked the idea of real mountaineering. On his last birthday we had climbed a little face, Ross roping with two friends and using all of my equipment. He was a very deliberate, safe climber and enjoyed displaying his acquired skills to his companions.

Glen was ambivalent. Our only joint climbing experience had been with our dog, Shanti, out at the practice face west of Victoria. Several groups were already there, doing the easy routes above Humpback Road. We climbed up a crack full of shrubs, Glen's red hair bobbing in an out of the brush ahead of me. But the exit was more difficult. I finally had to set the dog free and use her rope to secure Glen over a particularly airy cliff to safety. He never took much to climbing afterwards.

Ours was to be a simple hike to Kokanee Pass. The morning was cloudy as we headed up the trail, each with his pack, mine rather bulky with food, stove, and the tent. At the first small rain shower we inspected an old mine shaft, the rails curving deep inside the cliff. Together, the boys' imagination recreated scenes of miners pushing carts down to the shaft and back up full of gold.

During breaks in what was now intermittent drizzle, we hiked on through the tamarack, over a pleasant alpine meadow to Kokanee Lake. The trail crossed a boulder field skirting the west shore, then rose to the pass, to a vista I had seen during winter skiing. There the rain stopped.

While I set up the tent and cooked supper, Ross and Glen played in the heather below the hillock. Directly across the valley was my avalanche gully, less than two hour's hard walking. The ski pole must still be there. With only a bit of scrub growth on the slope it would still be visible. No summer trails passed that route; hikers would never see it. There was that same strong pull to the site—a desire for some completion to the incident.

Ross and Glen were playing trucks in the dirt outside a marmot's hole, but soon they would be tired and want to sleep. In four hours I could be back. But I could not go. Apart from all the creative mischief that two boys can devise, this was bear country. I put it off till the next morning.

During the night I was vaguely aware of rain on the

tent, but the noise diminished as I slept more soundly. With daylight, the sides seemed to be sagging. I pushed the tent away from Glen's bag and felt a heavy snow drift slide off the light nylon material.

This was August! How could it be snow? Ross had been sleeping against the tent wall; his bag also was soaked. Outside, a wind hissed through the trees projecting above the Pass. Everything was covered by a blanket of wet snow. Our stove, pots--any gear left outside the tent was buried. Around the edge of the thicket the wind was whipping the snow, covering the trails. The boys had boots and jackets, but we were ill-equipped for these conditions. This looked like a real scenario for hypothermia!

The porridge was soon boiling and the boys pried from their wet bags. Ross was fixed on staying there. His bag, even when wet, was more comfortable than the storm outside. I gave them breakfast inside the tent. If we waited a few hours, would we find the trail around the lake, or have to stumble through a mile of snow-covered boulders? Would we be stronger now than after a day and another night lying in wet bags? We were in a full-fledged summer blizzard. I had to forget about my ski pole; a forced march to the forest was needed--now!

With all the clothes available Ross and Glen dressed, then strapped on their packs with the now soaked sleeping bags. I packed up all of the gear I could find. While striking the tent, I sent them both over the hillock and down the trail, neither in a very positive frame of mind. In five minutes the tent was stowed in my pack, and I was off.

Just over the hill top, the wind hit me head-on. No more than ten paces out of the shelter of the trees, Ross and Glen stood huddled together against the cold wind and driving snow, crying.

Ross still wanted to go back and set up the tent; in his frustration he started shouting, blaming me for all the discomfort. He was hysterical and wouldn't listen. I slapped him across the mouth. That stopped the tirade, only to be replaced by screaming when blood trickled from his nose. I was angry, but more, I was scared. There was no possibility of carrying one boy, let alone two of them around the lake and into the protection of the forest. Now, I was panicked. Grabbing Glen's soaked mitt, I shouted above the wind.

"Just get on the trail in front of me and march!"

The north shore of Kokanee Lake was just visible. Slipping and stumbling over the rocky trail we were soon soaked to the skin. But gradually the crying subsided and our effort warmed us.

At the south end of the lake we halted. My emergency chocolate bars provided some additional energy and psychological value; a flicker of determination returned. We started to work together instead of each of us living in our discomfort, in our fear. In an hour we were back to the edge of the timber. It was still snowing heavily, but the wind was above the trees. The trail was visible and we knew it was now just a matter of an hour or so till we reached the shelter of the car.

Was, indeed, our situation as desperate as it seemed to me that day? Ross and Glen still wonder. I am surprised that I actually hit Ross--especially in the face. We've talked about it.

The ski pole continues to lie in an avalanche gully north of Kootenay Lake. These many years later, I doubt that I could find it.

--oo--

Mountains of Vancouver Island are not particularly dangerous. Not compared to the Rockies, where, as Don Vockeroth had said, "You had to hold the ridge together while you climbed it!" Of course, there is loose rock and melting snow; the gods conspire to throw the odd missive your way. But most of the dangers are subjective, problems you create by your very presence.

Mount Colonel Foster is the most difficult of Island peaks, a steep east face with ribs and gullies, a serrated summit ridge and a snow field approach to one end. But there is no easy way to the highest summit. I'd been near it once; Syd Watts had led a combined trip of the Alpine Club and the Island Mountain Ramblers to climb Mount Elkhorn. It was at least my third trip to Strathcona Park with Syd and John Gibson, an inseparable mountain duo who seemed to know every ridge and peak in the Park. It was a large party, so we split the party, five climbers to explore Rambler Peak at the top end of the valley, the remaining seven to Elkhorn. At dawn my contingent crossed the river on a log jam and headed up the forested bank toward Elkhorn.

When we exited the tall conifers, we were in the wrong gully, below the cliffs of the open plateau leading to the upper route. It was good for a young climber to know that even Syd could get lost. By now, he was pushing my active ambition and gave me the lead to climb a small roped pitch to the plateau. It went easily enough. As I belayed the rest up, I examined, across the valley, the east face of Colonel Foster, the morning sunlight playing on vertical ribs of the face. I knew that awful precipice had been climbed; the exposure must have been terrific, nearly a thousand metres above the lake. I could see attempting the summit, but doing it via the face was quite another matter!

"The mountain looked rather different before the earthquake in 1946." Syd explained as I photographed. "The whole north end collapsed and slid down the slope. See where the trees haven't grown back yet? The debris jammed the stream and formed that little lake; it's called Landslide Lake. Now, the easiest route is on the south end where the snow comes down to that narrow neck."

For the time being, our focus was Elkhorn. An hour higher, in the crack that forms the usual route to the summit of Elkhorn, we found a huge chock-stone. John tried a route under it while I climbed around the outside. Above, I clipped my climbing harness into the rope and John tied onto the other end. The rock was loose and our rope pulled off small stones, pelting the climbers below the chock. Syd decided to take the rest of the party down while John and I went on to the summit. Despite the hazard of loose rocks, I still preferred the psychological connection of the rope. The rest of our group below was now out of the crack and safe. There was no technical difficulty, but we continued carefully, balancing on the steep scree. In the rising cloud there was an eerie sense of isolation, no sound from our companions below, no horizon to provide orientation or balance. We made the summit in complete overcast, knowing we were there only because of the cairn.

Down-climbing the scree was far worse than coming up, but we escaped from the gully without taking any direct hits. The sharp reports of stones ricocheting far below proved Syd had been right to get clear. But Colonel Foster was still there as we descended below the clouds and through the forest. Serrated and brittle, the peak threw us a mocking challenge.

A year later, Dave and I hiked up the Elk River trail in a threatening drizzle, our attention fixed on the Colonel. Through the timber, along the rushing river and over the gravel flats we discussed our options. We weren't interested in the vertical topography of the east face. We hoped that the summit was accessible via the snow couloir Syd had pointed out. We decided to try this and called it the *hourglass* route. But the weather did not co-operate. The drizzle turned into rain as we passed the gravel flats and by the time we got the tent up at Landslide Lake it was a downpour. All afternoon, it came down. Tucked into our sleeping bags in the narrow tent, we discussed alternately the possibilities of the route and the probability of us returning to Victoria defeated. In the receding likelihood of a successful climb, we slept.

During the night we slept too soundly. The rain pelted down and wept through our tent's leaking seams. With the light of dawn it rained less and we cooked porridge from inside our damp bags, the stove just outside the flap. The clouds seemed to be lifting. We decided to go.

At the south end of the lake the polished rock slabs led up to frozen snow and we fixed our crampons. Near the neck of the hourglass there was a break where the snowfield tumbled over a four metre cliff, leaving a thin slab of ice projecting like a roof. Below the break was a crevasse where the snowfield had pulled away from the rock face, deep and dark and running with water. We roped up. Avoiding the overhanging roof to our left, we climbed the short rock cliff using the front points of our crampons.

Above the hourglass, we sped upward through the streaming fog into filtered morning sun, the snow hard and steep, in perfect condition all the way to the ridge. Avoiding the saw tooth ridge itself, we climbed on rotten rock onto the south east face, bypassing several gendarmes. By one o'clock, in blazing sunlight, we topped out on the sharp rock of the South Summit. Opposite, only a few metres higher, the main summit beckoned. But between lay some extremely messy climbing with vertical cliffs, broken slabs and loose rock everywhere. I reminded Dave of the aphorism;

"There are old climbers, there are bold.
But there are no old, bold climbers!"

Knowing that the hike down from the Lake would take at least three hours, the drive home five hours in the dark, and that we had to work the next morning in Victoria, we decided that, for practical purposes, we had climbed Colonel Foster.

I have often wondered about this decision. The summit always seems to assume greater importance than it should. We climb for a variety of reasons. Escaping urban sloth, we strengthen our manhood (or womanhood) and confidence in our own abilities. Wilderness travel is an uncertain "return to the hunter" from the lives of our ancestors. We experience the freedom and challenge in seeking the elusive summit. The fun, and the challenge too, is found in the climbing, not necessarily in standing on top. William Dalrymple in his book "In Xanadu" quotes Sir Richard Burton, "...how melancholy a thing is success. Whilst failure inspirits a man, attainment reads the sad prosy lesson that all our glories 'are in shadows not substantial things..' "

On Colonel Foster, at the point where we stopped there was still some tricky work to be done; we had not done all the climbing necessary to make the peak. How important is the summit and why is it so critical? Is it merely the "bragging rights" or is there something in the psyche, the necessary self-completion of the task? This dilemma is not unique to climbing. We set ourselves many objectives that defy rational consideration but, once decided, we hang onto the idea with unrealistic fervour.

We plunged down the snowfield in great humour. On reaching the hourglass we down-climbed the cliff, still with our crampons attached, and, reaching the lower snow, we removed the rope.

Just then, the thin ice roof above us broke off! Falling straight down, it struck our hardhats and exploded around us. I was stunned by the impact and grabbed my ice-axe just before it fell into the crevasse. We were badly shaken. I just stared down that bottomless black hole and felt the nausea rise. Descending the slabs I was still very unsteady. Gone was my earlier composure as I crab-crawled down slabs we had scampered up in the morning.

While tramping down the endless trail, Dave and I replayed the circumstances of such an accident. One of us might have been knocked into the crevasse. With the rope untied, perhaps even in the pack of the casualty, the results could have been fatal. The events at the hourglass were the focus of my private thoughts during the long hike down the Elk River valley, mostly in the pitch dark of a moonless night. That slab had been an objective hazard, one we could not have avoided. We had accepted the risk by climbing up and down under the roof. But in hindsight, we should have moved away from the cliff before we removed the rope.

Most of my climbing partners, especially Dave, seemed to be capable of taking these dangerous situations in stride. But not me. In the past I had been playing out my fear in other ways, substituting anger for a quiet acceptance of a dangerous event, blaming others for my own stupidity or fear, trying to rationalize, in hindsight, the risks we had taken. Now, I could voice my concern about circumstances I viewed as dangerous, and not just submerge my fear, disguising my real feelings to protect some macho image.

There were no recriminations here, I was starting to accept such occurrences. I was no longer on track to becoming a climbing icon, one that had to show invincibility in the face of danger. The horror of the black hole at the hourglass diminished on the long drive home, well into the early hours of morning. And when we met, in suit and tie at the office only a few hours later, we remembered mostly the exhilaration of the climb.

--oo—

Beyond Campbell River is another group of mountains, not high but challenging. Accessible from Kelsey Bay on the east coast, Victoria Peak is best known of these. Before the highway was completed to Port McNeil, the others in the group, Mounts Sutton, Schoen, Cain and Abel could be reached only from Woss Camp along a gravel road north from Gold River on the west side of the Island. In the fall, I went with Paul and Diane to attempt Mount Cain, which was unclimbed, we believed. New to the Island, this adventurous couple usually climbed alone, without any of the older, experienced climbers along. Paul had enough confidence to decide his own routes and Diane, small but wiry, had enough stamina to share them.

My old Chev van weathered the seven hour drive from Victoria and the logging road switchbacks up Cain Creek Road to almost the 1200 metre level. We ground to a halt at the end of the road among stubby conifers. While access to the mountain was great, we would rather have hiked up another 500 metres and seen these slow-growing trees saved. It would be many decades before replanting and regrowth could duplicate what had been there. (I have never been back; a ski development now replaces the lost forest. Maybe this was planned all along.)

From the campsite we climbed in the morning dew towards the skyline of the twin-peaked mountain. The day was grey, with mists coming and going around the peaks. Up the ridge we scrambled, using scrub juniper as handholds on the short rock pitches. We were on the first summit by eleven, peering out through the cloud at the grey form of "Brother Cain" to the east. We rested and ate a bit; then Paul explored the gap between. Through the fog, we could tell that the other side was marginally higher. As usual, we had no difficulty in climbing the easier and lower summit. We decided to down-climb into the gap and to try to find a route up the other peak.

I led down a steep crack. Diane followed, with Paul last on the rope, protecting our descent. It was extremely steep, with few holds, so we moved one at a time. About halfway down I set a piton so that Paul would have at least some protection for his descent. Reaching the bottom, I wondered how they would make it, first of all, Diane, with her short reach, and then Paul, lacking the security of a top-rope. Soon her yellow rain jacket and green hardhat appeared out of the crack; she traversed the face to the notch where I sat taking in rope. Paul followed. He took a long time, presumably using extreme care, pausing to remove the piton, the ring of his hammer echoing off both the peaks. Soon he also was down.

The dampness of the day contributed to our mood. Fog hung on both cliffs. We were intimidated by the steep rock on either side. The gap was electric. Everything you touched moved. With our noses rubbed up against Cain's main summit, it was clear to us that this was not a route we would be doing that day. The mountain was well named, the evil one of the two brothers. We all wanted to get out of the gap and back to camp.

Again I led off, this time down to the snowfield north of the col. The rock was covered with loose boulders; below it the snow sloped away steeply. But with the rain, the snow was softened and I could kick secure steps in the surface; immediately I felt the security of solid footing. Diane came down, reaching the margin of the snow.

Just then, a huge boulder between her and Paul started to move! He shouted; we both saw it coming. I was far enough away, but Diane was in a direct line. Ponderously, it rolled toward her. She couldn't jump out of the way, only duck down below the rock edge onto the snow. Just above her, it bounded over the lip onto the snow, grazing her pack and knocking her down into a small fissure, then fell back against the cliff, smashing her hand.

Quickly, I dug the snow away above her. She was clear of the boulder and only a metre below me. Paul was screaming and descending directly down the slope above us. I hollered that she was all right (though I was not at all sure) and that he should come down by our route.

Soon he was down and we both dug snow away.

Diane cried out in pain. There was blood splattered on the snow around her. But her legs were still working and she climbed up to us, clutching her hand and stumbling blindly. We were on a steep snow slope, but quickly got a pressure bandage onto the hand and tied it high on her opposite shoulder.

Diane was very unstable but she could walk. Normally quite confident, she had lost her sense of balance and with it, her usual composure. Clearly in pain, Diane was mostly afraid of the steep snow slope we had to traverse to the exit col. Paul kicked steps and stuck close to her, while I belayed with the rope from behind.

Somehow we got across to the col, through it and down the sidehill to our camp. Every step was an ordeal for Diane. She was losing blood through the bandage. Paul tightened it while I broke camp. Fortunately, the truck was only 400 metres below, down an easily graded meadow. I carried Diane's pack and Paul supported her. It seemed hours till we reached the road.

With all the events of the day, the down-climbing to the gap, the accident, the long traverse and descent, it was already six o'clock. And with the shortened fall days, dark would soon be upon us.

The branch road seemed full of pot-holes we hadn't noticed on the drive up. Even the main logging road was rough, with an accumulation of gravel on the corners, limiting our speed. Again, Paul tightened Diane's bandage, yet it continued to soak red, through and onto the shoulder of her shirt. By the time we reached Gold River the medical clinic was closed. The emergency call numbers were vague. So, together we agreed that an extra two hours on a paved road to the Campbell River hospital would serve Diane's needs better and we pulled back onto the highway.

The adrenalin was wearing off as we limped into town. The hospital duty doctor confirmed what we already knew--

that her hand was smashed, but that the bleeding had stopped. An hour later, Diane left "Emergency" with a Demerol high and an elbow-length cast. At the all-night diner, already she could laugh at her attempts to down Chinese food one-handed. Back onto the pavement again, we lasted only an hour en route to Victoria. Finding a beach-access road we stretched out in the van and soon were lost in healing sleep.

Using my own devices, my internal "guru-within" was not getting me onto many summits. But it was teaching me that there was more to a mountain than the pinnacle. On one level I had always known that, but now I believed it. I was becoming more self-critical, watching the action from "outside my head," even while it was occurring. It made a difference to my reactions. But I still had to rely more on my intuition.

It seemed that no mountain or climb was perfect. Colonel Foster's beautiful hard snow route had started and ended with a traverse under overhanging ice. The final few feet to the summit were blocked by a loose and jagged ridge. Mount Cain was strewn with precariously balanced boulders; in the col we all had a premonition of disaster. There was always a measure of risk in climbing, no matter how carefully we chose our routes and protected our passages.

The risk *did* add to our sense of adventure. It also made us appreciate life more--even later in the humdrum of the city. We reminded ourselves that there are risks everywhere, but in daily life they are often unseen. In mountaineering, you know they are there; you take as many precautions as you can, then you accepted the outcome. One of my old ironworker friends from an early bridge jobs had told me, "you just make it a little bit safe--then you take a chance!"

Life itself is unpredictable. To deal with its vagaries many fix their faith on an external God, others on themselves, with or without any supernatural power to assist. I hadn't come to any firm knowledge of where my own faith might be realized. I was looking at life, and death, a little more directly, starting to see that life would carry on after I had departed. I was just a minor biological event! Of course, my own life was dear to me. But, like the climbs I was making, it was the living that was important, not its culmination. Mainly, I wanted to experience life, and at the same time, give it meaning for me. What would give that meaning, or enhance it?

On Mount Cain, the adversity we shared, the help we provided to each other were the marks of that adventure. Constancy in the face of trials are powerful incentives to friendship. After that trip Paul and Diane were more than mere fellow-climbers.

The mountain was finally climbed from the south east in better weather, initially up a sloping snowfield, then later on rock, both avoiding the ominous gap between the peaks.

--oo--

Above me, they climbed where the snow ridge met the sky. My pack was far too heavy--I just couldn't hold their pace. Dave and Paul were ten years younger than I, but from three hundred metres behind it was difficult to remind them.

There were reasons to be tired. We had been up since 4:30 am for the black-of-night drive up-Island to Nanaimo to catch the Horseshoe Bay ferry. On the mainland we drove an hour along the highway toward the Whistler ski village, but before we reached it we turned onto the logging road north of the Cheekeye River. The snow was gone in the valley. We caught a ride in a logger's pick-up, bouncing up the rocky switchbacks to the 1000 metre level. There the road died and snow covered the ground. We strapped on our gaiters and prepared our packs. With our early start, there hadn't been any hurry. With two full days for Garibaldi Mountain, one to set camp high on Brohm Ridge and then, Sunday to do the climb and pack out, it was a typical climbing weekend.

Garibaldi had been a regular objective for mainland climbing clubs. First climbed in 1907 by a six member party, our climb wasn't going to be any first ascent, or even a new route—the Brohm Ridge and Warren Glacier route had been repeated many times since. Ours had none of the special categories that mountaineers create to make their climbs unique. But Garibaldi had been on our list for a long time; we had all tried before. The previous year, Dave had conducted a tour of the whole south face in a white-out, looking for a way past the precipitous maw of the bergschrund. Altogether, Paul and Dave had made five attempts from various directions and, usually because of bad weather, had not reached the summit. The boys were sore with failure.

An imposing snow peak, Garibaldi rises 2680 metres above the nearby tidewater. From the Dairy Queen in Squamish, gazing east over your peanut buster parfait, you see only the south peak, Diamond Head, twenty metres lower but a soaring pyramid, hiding the main summit. While often climbed, Garibaldi is challenging and a legendary magnet for bad weather. A gentle fog in the valley becomes a raging blizzard on her shoulders.

Climbing from the logging road towards Brohm Ridge, we ascended on spring corn snow through open timber. By 2 pm, we were above the ski lift where we would camp. A row of cable towers stretched down to a quaint log lodge. Apart from its newness it looked like most ski hills in summer--lacking any reason to be there. This one was doomed; a combination of financial woes and environmental outcry sealed its fate. Later it was totally removed.

It had already been a long day. It was a sparkling afternoon with a steady breeze. The sharp thrust of Diamond

Head periodically snagged a cloud from its eastward progress. I erected the tent and brewed soup. Dave and Paul, frustrated by bad weather so often in the past, worried that the wispy cirrus would bring a storm. When they started talking about the long evenings at this time of the year, I should have known what was coming. This trip had been their initiative--they did the planning, figured out the route; I was just along for the ride. So I yielded when, at 3 pm in perfect weather, they decided that this two-day mountain should be done in one.

Dave finally halted at the edge of the glacier to fit crampons to boots. The gap closed and I tied onto the pigtail of the climbing rope, forcing myself to keep up--to join the momentum of the others so as not to drag on the rope.

Passing several gaping cracks at the toe of the slope, Dave led up the steepness of the glacier, contouring right. The spindrift snow now swirled across the surface, filling our tracks. At the rear, I jammed bamboo-reed flags into the crust every rope length, leaving a trail we could find in a storm. Just below the apparent line of the bergschrund, we reached the right edge of the glacier. Dave tried the steep rock ridge. Exposed to the jet-stream wind sweeping the north face and finding no secure holds for climbing the icy rocks, finally he had to come down. It was now 8 pm. Retreat became inevitable, and we started to trudge down the track.

I was pretty satisfied that we had done our best, ready to leave it for another day. But Paul continued to glance over his shoulder up the sloping snow face. Finally, he spotted a snow bridge over the bergschrund leading directly to the upper snowfield.

"Reverse the rope; let's go for it!" he insisted. Dave agreed. By now my lethargy of the afternoon had dissolved in the steady rhythm of the climb up the glacier. Summit fever infected us all.

Being at the rear, I inherited the lead for the delicate passage. We did not know exactly where the bergschrund was located, but the whole area had a hollow feel. I spread my weight evenly on hands and feet, trying to ignore a mental picture of me swinging by the rope, suspended from the lip of the crevasse. The fragile crust held. The crux was behind us.

In just an hour of step kicking in the loose snow we reached Garibaldi's summit in the final glow of sunset. The strong wind still hammered the ridge. Surreal views expanded south across the Garibaldi Neve and beyond, where peaks thrust up through clouds, catching light from the speeding slant of the sun's rays. To the west was the long, triangular form of Mount Tantalus, with the red ball setting behind. And in the east, already the full moon was high.

This summit, the culmination of much mental and physical effort, was a momentary, but ecstatic spike in our psyche. Finally, a worthwhile summit. And we were in that unique time and place together. We were in a dream scene, poised above the dark void of the earth below. Even climbers in the Himalayas, at their absolute limit of endurance and in weather conditions where a fatal bivouac is a possibility, still report staying even an hour on the summit, so strong is the emotional release of arrival. Now, it was possible to believe.

In the hurrying dusk, Paul plunge-stepped straight down the fall-line, keeping the rope extended, hoping that if one of us dropped through the crust, that maybe the others could hold the fall. Soon he was past the bergschrund and led on down the windswept glacier into the closing darkness. Our ascending footprints were obliterated by the blizzard, but his intuition led him to the first of the snapping flags that marked our upward route. By linking flag to flag, we soon stepped off the glacier ice into the snow bowl, eerie in the rising moonlight.

We had come away from our camp as light as possible.

The food rations consisted of Dave's kilogram of trail mix and some dried fruit. Despite its boring sameness and the sticky globs of melted chocolate chips, it was now virtually gone. The canteens were dry. We were absolutely bagged. Flopping in the snow, we considered a diversion to the hut over on the Neve, two kilometres away. But, our chances of finding it at night were slim and we turned back towards Brohm Ridge.

Then the lights went out! On the ferry there had been talk of an impending eclipse of the moon. Then, it had been of no consequence to us. We had planned to climb our mountain in daylight, now we were forced to contend with total darkness.

We let our eyes adjust to the blackness and stumbled on. It had been 18 hours; most of that time we had been working hard. With the immense relief of making the summit and getting off the ice safely, we succumbed to our fatigue. First one would plump down, virtually unable to proceed. The other two would pick him up, get him moving, only to have another collapse.

As happens in the mountains, especially when fatigue deadens your ability to compromise, even good friends can disagree. Dave returned to the ridge to retrace our known ascent route around the snow bowl. Paul headed directly across the bottom, choosing to climb out at the far end. I found a compromise route, half way up the slope. Each felt his was the best line; triumphant calls to this effect echoed around the blackness.

Only an hour earlier we had shared an incredible summit. On the descent we helped each other fight the numbing fatigue; now, we were completely at odds. But, in the end our argument gave us back strength, an incentive for each to prove he was right. We were all headed for the same point on the ridge, each rushing to show that his route was shortest.

At the far end of the bowl our three trails converged.

By then, our conflict just didn't matter any more! Forgotten was the disagreement, the earlier rancour. I knew that fatigue was the source of my previous overreaction. The moon reappeared. The snow was hard and we walked together, not strung out in the usual mountaineering line. I felt the relief of knowing all the danger and struggle was past, that our camp was only a few more kilometres away.

At the tent we collapsed. In the snow-moon-whiteness, we realized this was a surreal scene that would endure in memory. We were too hyped up, too tired to just lie down and sleep. We dragged out the packs and cranked up the stove. After two cups of steaming soup, finally, we were able to focus on our sleeping bags. It was the sleep of the dead. Many hours later we woke in the noonday sun to the whine of skidoos burning donuts around our tent.

"Show me the man you honour and I will know what kind of a man you are, for it shows me what your ideal of manhood is, and what kind of a man you long to be." Carlyle

Outside the plane's window rock walls flashed by. Shreds of cloud hung on the ledges, but Robin could just see the postage stamp of a lake in the valley and he held the Otter in a tight spiral down between the cliffs. The centrifugal forces were terrific.

The same cliff came around again, appearing above Dave's shoulder, then passed the side window where Charles and Rick peered out. Then we were in cloud, thankfully soft-centred, then past the cliff again. Finally, the inward force reduced sharply; a level white horizon appeared straight ahead. The plane cleared the rubble at the end of Tellot Lake. Robin cut the power; the pontoons, banging against the ruffled water, slowed us to taxi speed just before the far shore.

Dave jumped out on the pontoon, stretched to a dry boulder and steadied the wing. By tailing the float plane into shore we were able to get our packs and our boots onto the moraine without dunking. With a final wave, Robin gunned the empty Otter clear of the lake and angled off towards Campbell River. We were alone at the bottom of the Tellot Glacier, south east of Mount Waddington and 250 kilometres north of Vancouver.

No sooner than our Otter was lost to our hearing, a Norseman seaplane appeared, touched down and delivered four Japanese and their gear onto the shore beside us. Charles and Rick helped them hoist their packs up the slope.

Then we all silently watched the Norseman disappear. The relief of the successful landings in such inhospitable surroundings expressed itself in nervous laughter. For a while we could hear the distant drone, then silence.

"Amazing," said Rick, "how fast they are gone, how quickly we lose our only link to civilization."

Our two parties had no common language, but the Japanese' actions indicated that they felt the same. We knew our expeditions had begun. Charles shared our fresh apples (heavy food) with our fellow-climbers. It was an unlikely coincidence that our two parties had arrived at the same time. We saw them disappear west over Nabob Pass toward the Tiedemann Glacier while we headed straight up the Tellot. A week later, when we were on our way out, their empty tents were still on the upper glacier, probably awaiting their return from Waddington itself.

This is a huge region, with sharp ridges and the troughs between, filled with wide, crevassed glaciers flowing south to Bute Inlet. Unlike the Japanese, we were not planning to attempt the summit of Waddington. We wanted to explore the area, to get a feel for the other peaks and snowfields. Of course, we hoped to climb something, but this was a mountain holiday, a getaway from the office.

The aura of these remote snowfields had been reinforced by tales spun by Don and Phyllis Munday, of their early days of discovery by sea access and by long wilderness trips up the western valleys. Not long before, I had met Phyllis at a mountain camp, then again at her Vancouver home, where she was enjoying an active old age, highly revered by all as Honorary President of the Alpine Club of Canada, living on memories of days in the snow and salal.

And Roger Neave had told me the details of his epic 1934 expedition to this "Mystery Mountain." At 4016 metres, this is the highest point in B.C.'s Coast Range, indeed, all of Canada excepting the Yukon. But more than that, it was then touted as unclimbable because of the extreme steepness of the rock and the severity of weather which plastered ice on the pinnacle year 'round.

With Campbell Secord and Art Davidson, Ferris and Roger Neave had driven from Winnipeg via the Crowsnest Pass (the Banff connection was not then available), north through the interior of British Columbia to Williams Lake, then west to Tatlayoko Lake. By horse to begin with, then mostly on their own backs, they ferried their supplies down the Homathko River, despite swollen glacial creeks and impassable gorges which forced the party to detour, in some cases right out of the valley, using up to three relays to get all of their gear to base camp.

On the actual mountain, they pioneered the route most often used today, climbing the Tiedemann Glacier and the broken Bravo Glacier to the Spearman Col, then traversing to the final rock pinnacle. Using a three man home-made sleeping bag and no tent, the team was forced to halt two days at the col because of poor weather while Davidson, waiting at base camp, could only speculate on the whereabouts of his companions. Dwindling provisions encouraged them to attempt the summit on the third day.

Cutting ice from each rock handhold was laborious and the rock afforded no opportunity to anchor the rope. Though they made good progress on the north side of the pinnacle to a point less than 100 metres short of the summit, they were forced to retreat in a blizzard, spending the night in a crevasse to escape the storm, then probing their way in a white-out back to camp in the morning. The descent of the Bravo Glacier, now laden with fresh snow, was fraught with avalanche peril, but they finally returned to base camp safely.

Their pioneering information assisted the subsequent successful climb by Fritz Weissner and Bill House which reached the summit in 1936. But the Neaves' attempt on Waddington had been a magnificent achievement in difficult conditions and very nearly resulted in the first ascent.

Perhaps all of this foreknowledge of the difficulties of the Waddington region was counterproductive. We were keen to see and come to grips with the spectacular mountains, but we knew how vast the region, how isolated we were, how intimidating the peaks themselves, the reason, perhaps, why we came over-prepared. At the moment of starting, we knew we had too much gear. Each pack weighed 30 kilograms or more: climbing hardware, two ropes, food, stoves and fuel, sleeping bags and personal gear. And the big "Mount Logan" tent. Most of our climbs from the hut would be day trips. Certainly, we hoped to get up to the Plummer Hut by nightfall. But that couldn't be guaranteed. Also, the outbound trek involved at least one night. (Robin was to fly into Ghost Lake, farther down the valley from our drop-off point, where his Otter could take off fully loaded. At Tellot Lake, he had to be empty to get off.)

With these unaccustomed packs we staggered up the scree to the lateral moraine at the glacier edge. With all of us roped against the possibility of hidden crevasses, Dave led off. The surface snow was soft but firm immediately under. Crampons were not necessary as the middle of the glacier was relatively flat. My chest harness was a bit snug, but connected to a pair of leg loops it was a secure tie-in method, one that was likely to keep me (and my heavy pack) upright if I fell into a crevasse. Charles insisted on his Whillans *sit-harness* attached to the rope at the belt buckle; hopefully its stability would not be tested by a fall.

The lower Tellot Glacier is relatively flat, but it stretches endlessly toward the high mountains east of Mount Waddington. Then comes the steeper icefall, leading up and around Claw Peak to the hut. Dave held to a steady pace despite the hot July sun. The jagged granite spires on our left and the glaciated walls on the right bracketed the glacier, increasing the effect of snow-reflected sunlight. We plodded on through midday and into the early afternoon, getting continuously wetter from our exertions and the heat. When we rested we dropped our packs where we stood, keeping the rope strung out and with several metres between each climber. But getting the loads back up was a major exertion, so that in the end the rest stops became fewer and fewer.

The weaving route through the transverse crevasses increased as the glacial surface steepened. Our route reminded me of a snake; our rope twisted around crevasses that split the glacier into sections; together I had the impression of a snake's body. The yoga symbol of the "Cobra," a Hatha yoga pose, related on many levels to our meandering climb. The Christian connotation of the snake is one of evil, although in India, while feared, it is viewed as a majestic and powerful creature. Our careful detours from a direct ascent line emphasized the presence of physical danger and a need for care and self-control. I became aware of the snake, aware of its threat.

Approaching the icefall, the snow became deeper on top of the glacier ice and Dave was obviously tiring. We switched the lead and I kicked steps up several benches--ledges that we knew to be disguised crevasses. As soon as the sun dropped behind Claw Peak the temperature plummeted. Supper time passed, but still we hoped to make the hut before dark. We munched trail mix and continued. The angle of the slope steepened further. Here the ice squeezed through a narrower gap like frozen rapids. The edges of the glacier appeared even steeper so we kept to the middle. I had to use my iceaxe for stability; kicking each step into the bank kept me warm. However, the others were suffering; Dave held the rope limply, standing like an automaton, huddled against the cool breeze. I kicked up the slope even faster, but at the top of one step my axe punched right through the lower lip of a wide crevasse, one extending right across the slope. We were not going to make the hut that night!

Back down on the bench, it was clear that Dave was in trouble. He just stood there, seemingly unaware of what was happening. Exhausted from the day's leading, losing body heat in the cool wind, he was becoming hypothermic. Despite the slope, we decided to camp right there. Charles and Rick levelled a tent platform and got the Logan tent upright; not a pretty job, but shelter. While the stove roared, heating water, Dave slumped on his pack, his sleeping bag around his shoulders.

He was able to eat some soup. Then we stuffed him into his sleeping bag in the tent. In failing light we all gobbled some reconstituted freeze-dried stew and followed him in. Maybe we were all a little hypothermic; I remembered nothing till waking with the dawn, finding all of our gear in a jumble hanging over the ledge at the bottom of the tent, tugging at the rest of us. But we had all recovered, especially Dave. We sorted the gear and stoked our own internal furnaces with oatmeal and brown sugar.

Dave led off again, finding a route to the left of the huge crevasse, eventually discovering a soft snow bridge that held while each of us crossed, right under the cliffs of Claw Peak. At the top of the icefall, the wind was strong in our faces. But by noon the silver walls of the Plummer Hut came into view.

Inside, we found it well-stocked with a tight-sealed food box filled with the leftovers from many climbing parties. Had we known, our packs could have been much lighter. As it was, our week at the hut was a gastronomic delight, with jellies and seasoning added from the stock, supplements to our austere menu of dried soups, freeze-dried entrées, rice and rye crisps. Spiced garlic sausage and cheese served us for lunches. Dave, the "Brit", had chosen the cheese. The rest of us, with Canadian cheddar tastes, complained bitterly at the four pounds of Cheshire, but ate it anyway.

Outside, we were overawed by the immensity of our surroundings. For the first afternoon we gazed across the glacial trough of the Tiedemann Glacier to the sharp summit of Waddington, distracted by the sporadic, booming avalanches firing down the east wall of Mount Munday. From our rocky viewpoint it appeared that the Bravo Glacier, the usual access to Waddington, was also under fire from the Munday "shooting gallery."

I knew that we had no plans for Waddington itself. Our nearest approach would be on our route out the Tiedemann Glacier, where it was wide, flat and safe. But these natural hazards were so pervasive, so dangerous; this whole region was so huge and so remote. Here, we saw no evidence of man's small victories over nature that give us so much comfort in the cities. But there was the opportunity to reflect on these awful surroundings and our insignificant place among them.

Swami Radha had explained that the yogic Cobra pose and the cobra itself symbolised temptation, not necessarily fear. She often referred to symbols to make an emotional impact. We are more attached to our personal symbols than we realize, and if we understand why they have such power over us, then we can free ourselves from unwanted or outdated ideas.

If I did not yield to temptation it would make me stronger in myself. Did that apply to mountains? Could I discriminate between real danger and my irrational fear, between ego-goals and climbs that were real spiritual progression? Was the cobra tempting us to do climbs beyond our abilities? Could I learn wisdom in yogic symbols that would help me to understand my mountaineering? Or would I have to discover my own symbology of the mountains?

Our first peak was unnamed and easy, a first ascent because no one had bothered with it before. Rick named it "Nandel," which translates roughly from the German, to "Little Sister." Later, on our second summit, Mount Argiewicz, we peered down the Radiant Glacier which dived to join the lower Scimitar glacier, itself dropping in a sweeping curve from the north side of the Waddington col. Despite our early start we waded crotch-deep in sun-softened snow the last hour home. The next morning we struck out toward the Tellot Spires. As we neared the peak, I found the thrusting granite blocks intimidating, and the access to them even more daunting. The route to the base of the rock required cutting steps in the snow directly across a ravine that had its bottom on the Radiant Glacier, several hundred metres directly below. Above, the climbing looked *hairy.* Dave was game, but I was choked by the danger of the climb in such an isolated landscape. Nothing emphasized more, our need to be totally self-reliant here.

Leaving the Spires unclimbed, we settled for the easier Tellot Peak, with good snow climbing and a granite block at the summit. It was a satisfying objective for all of us and Dave hardly grumbled at his loss of the Spires. Descending, we crossed to the Serra peaks. Even the smallest of the Serra peaks appeared a major undertaking, with steep rock slabs and a pyramid peak. It may have been within our capabilities, but we bypassed it on the way to the cabin, again wading in bottomless snow.

Rick ordered a victory banquet. I filled the huge Coleman cookstove that Charles had packed in. It used a pump, enabling quicker cooking than my small, slow, (and light) Optimus stove. But I hated the damn thing and it knew it. It was necessary to flood it to get a proper start. The spillage on the cook shelf went unnoticed until the stove ignited and with it a major conflagration. Charles grabbed the burning Coleman and pitched it outside while the rest of us shovelled snow onto the pool of burning gas. It was a near thing.

Clouds again surrounded the promontory in the morning. Dave and I tried a route on Claw, but chilled by the blowing mist and unable to judge our progress in terms of the whole peak, we retired to the dubious reading available in the hut. Charles was well into a National Lampoon magazine.

Descending from the Plummer Hut to the Tiedemann Glacier is not technically difficult, but our packs were awkward and the snow was already unstable. Our traverses cut the soft crust; the surface sloughed off, flowing like white water over the rocks and down the slope below us. Still, we descended to the Tiedemann without incident and prepared for the long hike out to Ghost Lake.

The lonely tent of the Japanese perched at Rainy Knob, waiting for its owners who must have been far above. By the looks of the weather they should have been attempting the summit that day. If anyone of our party begrudged them the mountain, they did not express it. We had found enough excitement on the easy peaks.

We plodded south for three hours dragging the mandatory rope. The direct sun and the reflected glacial heat cooked us; the fireworks avalanching off the high snowfields to the west prevented boredom. Internally, I was evaluating our marginally successful first expedition, still feeling overwhelmed by nature, now more than ever in awe of Roger Neave's early attempts on Waddington. We had travelled safely through isolated mountains and glaciers; we had suffered no injuries and we had all been inspired by the experience.

Our indirect, snake-like routes up and down the glaciers were like my halting approach to mountaineering. My path had been circuitous, my objective undefined. I had been trying to avoid danger, gradually understanding the physical skills needed, slowly accumulating the experience to accept new challenges, sometimes developing an internal calmness, self-control. More important, I was focusing on the type of objective I wanted. It was a very indirect and unplanned process.

Swami Radha had also symbolised the cobra as wisdom. To do the Cobra asana, you lie face down, slowly lifting your head, then successively raising each vertebrae of your spine into an upward curve. A very slow deliberate movement. Wisdom, too, arrives in a very circumspect manner, without announcing its presence.

Next morning, we grunted up the west shoulder of Mount Jeffrey. Near the top a cairn marked another passage, a climber had been killed while attempting the Bravo Glacier route to Waddington. This memorial was in an unbelievable spot. Behind us, the main peak of Waddington collected fleeting clouds like a plume. The Tiedemann Glacier, bracketed on both sides by sky-piercing peaks, was a wide, white avenue leading to the ramp of the Bravo, itself the obvious staircase to the upthrust of the Waddington massif. It was a glorious viewpoint, though it reminded of yet another mountain death.

Ghost Lake was our rendezvous point with Robin and his plane. To reach it we still had to circumvent an icefall and plunge-step down the long snow slopes east of Jeffrey. The trek out had been draining, done with still rather voluminous packs. But finally, we could descend into delicious green.

In the land of black and white, we had forgotten about growing, living things--like, for example, mosquitoes.

--oo—

Somewhere toward morning, I knew something was up. Now and then, a trickle of water would run down the tarp and into the cuff of my sleeping bag. I realized it was more than condensation, but sleep was so deep it was a subconscious awareness. I pulled the cuff tighter, rearranged my spine to avoid the rocky spurs poking up through the ensolite pad and ignored the world outside my bag.

Maybe an hour later I was roused again, this time by

cursing from the other side of the ridge where Jim and Rafe were bedded down between the rocks. Coming up for air, I sensed a new dawn. With it came a change in texture, with all sound muffled, perhaps by the heavy cloud almost within reach. Rubbing my eyes, I looked over to Rafe's bag.

"Christ, we're dumped with snow!" My words shattered the silence.

Rafe's head poked out from under his tarp. "You've just figured that out? I've been mopping up for the last three hours. Let's wake these guys and get back down the mountain. We're sure not going up the ridge when it's plastered."

My body ached from yesterday's effort of getting the camp up here, from the cramped sleeping position on my rocky bed. I had been in great shape coming to the Stikine region of northern British Columbia. We had packed the first loads up to the cache, then decided that it might be necessary to get out onto the snow face. I had gone down again, this time to get the crampons that we would need to grip the frozen morning snow. An extra three hundred metres down, then I shouldered my pack and humped back up to join the other three at the cache. Roger's crampons were steel, they felt like cast iron. Mine were "chrome-moly" alloy steel, lightweight and almost new; Roger's were heavy, but had seen over 40 years of service.

At dusk an incredible sun had set far out over the Pacific--a clear sky without a hint of trouble. This had been our second try at the ridge. And still we didn't even know if the route would go.

The Stikine is guarded from the sea by the Alaska panhandle; we had "choppered" in from Petersburg. Now, descending the scree of the ridge yet again, we looked south across the Dawes Glacier to Kate's Needle and the Devil's Thumb projecting above sharp-toothed ridges, marching in rows towards us from the sea. Behind us, Mount Noel rose to three thousand metres, still unclimbed.

Mount Ratz, just east of us, had been climbed by the legendary Fred Beckey, who owns more first ascents than anyone else in the Pacific Northwest. But we had our own legend with us. Roger Neave's courageous attempt on Mt Waddington in 1934 had set the stage for a long and brilliant mountaineering career. Now 71, Roger was rightly respected by the whole alpine community.

At 40, I was dubbed "Boy!" of the party. Rafe and Jim, both lawyers, were approaching 50. Jim was quiet; Rafe was experienced and ebullient. At times, it seemed he was trying to intimidate the mountain. I had only been climbing a few years and deferred to their experience, hoping I could do what I had to, or to have the clarity to say, "That's enough for me; I stop here!"

It stormed all through that night. We took turns crawling out of our big Logan tent, anchoring the guys against the wind, tying down the tarp on our supplies. When, in the morning, it finally played itself out, so were we.

In the afternoon the barometer started rising, and Roger and I skied around to Noel's south face. We could see another route--up a long snow gully on the upper glacier to the bergschrund, then slanting left across the face around and below the black pyramid which was the summit. It appeared feasible to climb it in one long day.

We sat on the rocks on the edge of the glacier, warmed by the intermittent sun. I knew Roger by his climbing record, but only slightly as an individual. In fact, I was surprised and honoured to be invited along. I'd not met Jim before, but Roger and Rafe were known by their travels. They had been in Peru, climbing in the Cordillera Blanca together. Roger had shown his slides to the local chapter of the Alpine Club of Canada. His high, hesitant voice reflected shyness; his understated descriptions of demanding climbs indicated a studied modesty. But also, pride was evident. Even he measured his success by the reaction of his audience.

In contrast, here he was natural, completely in his element, assessing only the private validity of the venture, only his own response to the task. Evaluation of success, whether by himself or others, would come later.

We left before daybreak. I remember the steady rhythm of our step, the crunch of our crampons on the firm early morning snow, the subdued light of a clear sky before the sun arrived and the slithering of the rope dragging along the crust. Rafe led; I was last, the four of us each spaced about 15 metres apart. We were connected together, yet separate enough to be alone. I was nervous, anticipating the difficulties, but glad finally to be making a summit drive. Before the bergschrund we threaded through seracs, melting towers of broken-off glacier, big as houses.

The sun was on us at the bergschrund and Rafe, stripped to his undershirt, led to the right where the glacier steepened, leaving a narrow bridge to the upper snowfield. Now on the steeper face, Rafe had to kick his crampons into the icy runnels where sliding snow had polished the ice. Roger enlarged the steps for Jim and me. I worried about the fresh snow sloughing off, sliding down past us. The sun was doing its work.

We all realized we were going too slow. Rafe was soon tired by the work. But to let someone else lead, to rearrange the rope on such a steep face was out of the question. So we switched leaders, end-for-end, placing me in front. I remembered our Garibaldi climb, where I had taken the lead, also by default. My luck had held then.

We headed across to the west to intersect a major rock rib, hoping to get out of the way of the snow slides and to gain the ridge in this way. As I led I watched the fresh snow sliding down, mostly in little snowball fans. No real problems. But it was hot and the runnels were lively. I came to one about eight metres wide, checked above and quickly started across.

Somewhere between here and there, I felt a rain of ice pellets. It felt like the start of a major avalanche.

I was thrown down the slope, successively jerking Jim from his belay, then Roger, then Rafe. Despite my hardhat, I lost consciousness. I "came to" while alternately flying through the air and bouncing down the ice. My axe was still tied to my wrist and I jammed in the pick. The rope yanked me off. Again I tried. Again I was plucked off and sent tumbling. Finally, my third self-arrest held and I stopped.

Jim was below me on the taut rope, just above the lip of the bergschrund. Roger was nowhere to be seen. Rafe was below, having shot right across the gaping crack.

Jim screamed at me: "Let me down, I can't breathe!" I was finally stopped and the panic started. I wasn't moving anywhere. I could see Jim all twisted up in the rope. I was afraid he would fall into the crevasse and pull me with him.

But Rafe was now on his feet and directing traffic from below. "Just back down a few feet, Gil. Jim, can you stand on your crampons? Untie and jump across to me here; I've got to dig Roger out. He's in the snow in the bergschrund." So I slowly relaxed my rigid fingers on my axe shaft, backed down and released Jim from his agony.

Roger had fallen head-first into the soft snow in the crevasse, inadvertently but effectively anchoring the lower part of the rope and stopping Rafe. I jumped down as Jim and Rafe hauled Roger out by the feet. "I couldn't tell which way was up!" Roger sputtered and cleared the snow from his goggles. Here below the bergschrund we were safe, at least temporarily. Most slides would dump their load into its gaping maw and not harm us.

We took stock. Mine was our only ice axe, still tied to me by my wrist loop. Jim had lost his down jacket out of his pack, Rafe, his camera. Otherwise we were all right. It was incredible that no one had broken anything or been cut by his or someone else's crampon spikes. My attempted arrests had kept the rope strung out. Looking below us, maybe another 50 metres down the slope, the glacier spilled over a rock bluff, God knows how high. Rafe borrowed my axe and climbed up to retrieve Roger's axe. It was sticking out of the snow above us, the strap hanging broken.

I wanted to get off the mountain, to escape to the safety of the glacier base camp. I was all for heading down right away. Roger was checking our route options. "The gully we came up is the funnel for all this loose snow," he said. "It's an avalanche track by now. We're probably better to get over onto the west ridge."

Rafe arrived back. "Don't worry, Gil. The mountain has spared us because she favours our advances. She is just flirting with us." If this was a comment on the whims of the mountain gods, I was not yet ready to hear it. I had lost interest in the summit; I was keen on a safe and early exit. Jim, happy to be able to breathe freely again, had a similar view.

But we both were silent, deferring to Rafe's confidence and Roger's experience. Besides, I had to agree, our rational choice was straight up to the rock rib which deflected snow slides from above, and from there to gain the ridge. But rational or not, in my heart I wanted to go down.

We split into two ropes, Roger and I together, to climb the mixed snow and rock terrain. It was slow climbing, but safe from the slides, with no runnels to cross. The rock, as always appearing easier from below, was very difficult when we were actually on it. Despite the skill of Rafe and Roger leading the ropes, the mixed snow and rock meant that belaying was difficult and rope-handling complicated. We had to regain height lost in the fall, then climb the steeper ground above. Time ground by. Finally, we reached the ridge about 6 pm, seven hours after the avalanche had hit us.

Now we were left with the choice. Up to the summit?

Or down the rocky ridge? We straddled the airy col as we would a bony-backed horse and considered our options. We were on a knife edge west of the summit and only two sharp pinnacles separated us from the top. We might be able to bypass the lower pinnacle, but we could not see the upper one or the summit block itself. Moreover, we were tired. The accident had taken its toll. And the escape route down the long, intricate ridge was still unknown.

Rafe, as always, was optimistic. "We've come this far; I think we should have a go at the summit."

I had been expecting the inevitable decision all afternoon, trying to assess the risks objectively. Was the wisdom of the cobra the fear that always tries to avoid danger? Or was the summit the snake's temptation, the unknown and waiting trap?

Finally, I voiced my opposition. After a whole afternoon of struggling with the question, I was not for taking any more chances. We had expected it to be a long climb, even without the tumble down the face! By adding the summit ridge to an already arduous day, we were stretching the limits. I had a vision of freezing to death trying to get down the ridge in the dark and did not want to add any more distance between us and safety.

"I'm going to eat before I vote." Roger pulled some flattened sandwiches from his pack. It had been about nine hours since our last hurried bite. None of us were willing to break Roger's silence. I made myself as comfortable as I could, making sure not to drop anything down either side of our steeple. Roger had his railroader cap down to shade the slowly sinking sun and perhaps to avoid our eyes. His greying stubble emphasized his age. He looked drawn, concentrating his attention on his food. He knew, with the vote already two to one; the crucial decision was his alone.

Finally, he began to repack his rucksack. "It seems to me that we may be close to the summit, but there are still two gendarmes to get around. It may be two, three hours till we get back here. Then, we have no idea of how this ridge will go, until we reach the cache. I think we have to go down now." The vote was three to one; Rafe did not object.

The ridge was badly broken and not at all direct. Rafe and Jim's rope was cut on three separate occasions by rockfall and had to be knotted together. In failing light we tried to rappel into a gully we hoped would lead to easy ground. It did not; we had to regain the ridge and continue painfully down. By 11:30 pm we could see the holds no longer. So we had to bivouac, without tarps or sleeping bags, sitting side by side on a ledge.

We were very thirsty; on the sharp ridge there was no access to the snow. The temperature hovered around freezing. We were all extremely cold, especially Rafe, who elected to sit separate, there being room for only three on the ledge. We used my small groundsheet as a makeshift tent. But two days of good weather finally strung together and the night was calm and without snow.

The bivouac hours were endless despite the extreme exhaustion I felt. I retraced the day and the preparations that had brought us to this point, the personalities of my mates and how we all fit into the expedition. Each of us sat and dosed in our little capsule of space, cold and uncomfortable, just waiting for daylight.

My thoughts went to Jean and our boys, wondering how they were managing. I had been away a lot, on business and climbing, and I knew Jean was having to deal with home and family (with the daily disasters created by two boys.) Between us, things had not been going well. Fortunately, we were out of the "quiet times," when we both existed in our own world and could not seem to break out, or even to define the reasons for our depression. The ashram time had helped. More than the Hatha yoga, the introspective workshops and the discipline of regular practice had helped us both. It took us out of the little problems of daily life, helped us to look beyond, to our real ideals and objectives, not just succumbing to the stresses of daily living.

After my own sojourn at Yasodhara Ashram, I had opened my mind to some of my shortcomings and enabled me to define my own life priorities. I should really be at home, getting on with these. But this invitation had come from Roger, the opportunity formed its own urgency. I could not pass it up.

At four o'clock we could move again. Through the crisp, cool morning we descended the fractured ridge, choosing the wrong route, climbing back up, trying another. The key to safety was Roger's patience; he would not let the extreme awkwardness of our position panic him. He was visibly worn from the strain of the climb and the long hours sitting waiting for the dawn.

It was two in the afternoon when the ridge became recognisable and our previous campsite hove into sight. Going straight for the food bag for anything juicy, we dug out the Spanish onions and ate them like apples.

"Tomorrow's task is to plunge into the unknown by yourself... You may gather the power needed to unfold the wings of your perception and fly to that infinitude." *Carlos Castaneda*

In March of 1979 an eclipse of the sun--the total darkness, the umbra--would pass over Portland, Oregon. Why not combine a climb of nearby Mount Hood and observe the event? The scientist in Rob (an ocean chemist) brought him along. Diane, just finishing a consulting job for some government department, needed a break. Rick, a government map-maker, and I had climbed a couple of the western volcanoes, Baker and Rainier, and had talked of working our way, mountain by mountain, down to St. Helen's, Adams, Hood, and even Shasta. (Within a year, St. Helen's had blown her own volcanic top off and the remaining cauldron was not in the least aesthetic.)

So we four crossed on the ferry from Vancouver Island and started the long drive to Portland. We discovered in my pack a paperback of Robertson Davies' novel, "Fifth Business." Rob started by quoting aloud poignant passages, familiar descriptions of life in rural Canadian villages. I was lifted back to my childhood town on the prairies, to the blend of farm and ramshackle village, to complicated people games, to the mystery of adult society seen by a boy's eyes. Soon we were reading everything aloud; first Rob, then Diane, then I would do a chapter. The reading rotation stopped with Rick who preferred to drive and listen. In the end we all arrived at the mountain, contented, the book half done, but with the weather steadily worsening.

Rather than setting up a tent in the darkness and the wind-driven snow that greeted us at the Phlox Point Campground, we slept in the van. Diane was short enough for the single cross-seat and the wooden equipment boxes formed an acceptable deck for the rest of us.

When the morning light hit the van we came to life, not in the world of Davies' novel, but in a snow-covered and deserted mountain campground. The snow had ended with the darkness. We fired up the Primus stove, doused our granola and milk powder in hot water. No cooking needed.

The weather had improved; patches of sun and cloud moved steadily from west to east. After packing up, we drove the last bit up to the Timberline Lodge at 1860 metres. This is the take-off point for summer hikers; the Timberline *is* Mount Hood. Here, the Pacific Coast Trail joins the Timberline Trail on the south side of the mountain, joins the host of summer hikers booting their way around Mount Hood. But then on the north west flank the trails separate, the PCT descending northward toward the "Bridge of the Gods" over the Columbia River.

In winter, Hood is somewhat a different matter. While the mountain is not technically a difficult climb, it is subject to the vagaries of west coast weather, with big dumps of snow above 1500 metres and regular white-outs when the moist Pacific air strikes its icy mass. Nowadays, it has two end-to-end tows and a regular following of downhill skiers. Then, there was only the single T-bar, mainly for beginners.

We organized our gear, locked the van and headed for the lift. By using skis and the T-bar we gained an easy 300 metres elevation. Where the lift topped-out the cloud was now solid fog and we were in it. There was no attendant at the top bullwheel. The silence was eerie, broken only by each T-bar as it rattled around the wheel, an intrusion from a technological world somewhere outside our fogbank. Visibility was about ten metres. Nowhere could we see the "Warming Hut" as noted on the maps, so we followed a row of red marker tapes fluttering from bamboo wands. Two hundred metres from the bullwheel we set up a tent to wait.

In the muffled sounds and half-light I wondered how

this trip would play out; "would we see the eclipse or our summit?" The fog was a factor. Usually, a climber views the mountain from a distance, then finds the base, the routes and paths to seek the mountain's summit. Without visibility, more intuition is needed. The heart of a mountain is not always the summit. There is often a place of decision, of protection, or of security in the face of the elements. And one can discover the mountain's essence or one's place in the adventure simply by experiencing that time and place.

Among yoga postures, the "Mountain" is often the closing stance, or asana, of a given sequence. To the uninitiated, one appears only to be standing. But it is a posture for centring, for stilling the mind using the flow of the breath as a focus. Seems simple, but this one posture was the basis for a two day workshop at the Yasodhara Ashram. The teacher later characterised the Mountain Pose as an introspective analogy to all mountains. Visualisation of the mountain's physical form as a representation of the spirit could bring centredness to life. Her metaphor came through the mists to the flanks of Mount Hood.

The mass and enduring quality of our mountain was a component, although with a volcano one cannot always be certain. The physical mountain was masked by weather; we were prevented from exploring its routes for the present. This would not necessarily destroy my experience. A climb in which the summit is achieved is often a climb with no learning. If the objective is reached it means that the weather is accommodating, the routes are straight-forward, the climbers prepared. It's the epics that are life-changing.

The slog up the Palmer glacier, the crossing to the White River snowfield, threading through the snow cliffs and crater rocks to the 3450 metre summit is not a demanding climb in summer. But this was still March and we were weekend climbers who lived at sea level. We had come up the lift early, hoping to climb to the 2600 metre level to shorten Sunday's climb. Now it seemed that we would be lucky to have even one clear climbing day.

There is only so much time to be spent in setting up a tent, arranging foam pads and sleeping bags and organising a cooking pit in the drifts outside the flap. Then, especially in a white-out with nothing to see, boredom sets in. Rob and Rick started roaming around on skis; soon we all trooped off to the east, following the row of fluttering ribbons. Fifteen minutes from our tent Rob found the missing "Warming Hut" looking badly drifted in and not at all warm.

Glad of our chosen camp location we skied back to the tent, groping up and down bumps, trying, with no horizon, to maintain balance. Just before the tent we found a cornice, maybe two metres high, where the snow had drifted to a peak. Below, the snow was like goose down. Diane marked the top with two tape-wands and Rob trampled an approach run a few metres up the slope above the cornice.

Taking turns, we skied down the runway, jumped as we passed the flags and enjoyed moments of weightlessness before coming back to earth in an explosion of powder, flailing skis and poles. To try this blind space flight once was to become an addict. We fed our habit. Only after several hours, with a strong twinge developing in my lower back, did I recover some sense and "kicked my monkey."

By now Rick had found another drift, this one solid-packed, and was digging away at the side with his avalanche shovel. When I found him only his feet protruded through a small hole, half a metre square. Mounds of snow flew out from between his legs, as a dog digging for a lost bone. Diane and Rob took turns enlarging the interior, while I alternately groaned about my back pains and shouted helpful hints above the noise of the rising wind. Digging a snow cave was a new experience for all of us even though we had all read the basic manual. As we usually climbed near sea level, we seldom saw dry snow. The diggers worked their way inside the drift, carving a low tunnel, then a step up to a sleeping platform, and finally, a rounded roof about a metre above the platform.

"That looks pretty wide, Rick," I called, when they eventually stopped shovelling and let me in the opening. "Don't you need more of an arch shape?"

"Damn engineers; no work, just advice," he countered. "There's no problem, at least a metre more snow above the ceiling. And it is harder than hell, judging by the digging."

It looked comfortable. Rick had his headlamp on, but enough light came in the door below us. With four bodies inside it was cramped just sitting there. But with the blizzard getting up, it would be warmer and quieter in the cave.

"How many can sleep inside?" Diane asked.

Rob stretched out on the platform. "Room for two. We should stick a ski pole through the wall for a ventilation hole. Put a candle in that little alcove. It'll be real cosy."

But if Rob was comfortable, Rick was not. After doing most of the digging, he was popping in and out of the tunnel, obviously very unhappy about being so confined. His claustrophobia invited some ribbing about someone who digs caves for other climbers to use!

Though Rick was younger than I, he had climbed more. His personality had developed with his climbing, and over the years I had watched as he dived into cycling and weight lifting, watched him change from a scrawny kid to a man with the biceps and pectorals needed for the pull-ups on vertical rock faces. Actually, his best love was ice climbing on frozen waterfalls and he searched all summer for suitable winter venues. As I lost the competitive urge and looked for easier climbs, Rick continued to drag me out for challenging ones, leading the hard bits to prove they were not difficult. It was like a reverse mentorship; I had opened some climbing doors for him and he wouldn't let me retire.

But Rick had never slept in a cave before, and wasn't about to start with this one. So the remaining three of us flipped pot lids; Rob lost. He and Rick rolled out their beds in the tent, while Diane and I funnelled our foamies and bags through the snow cave entrance.

Back outside, the tent was starting to drum a high-pitched staccato and the daylight was slipping away. Cooking was tricky. Once we got the stove going it chugged along; soon a few freeze-dried "cardboard" steaks were swimming in a foul brown liquid emulating gravy. With a mountaineer's disdain for his palate, Rob smacked his lips and called for more.

Our climb of Hood was now becoming a doubtful issue. With the solid cloud we'd had all afternoon, we wondered about even seeing the eclipse next morning. But the day had been great fun; we had enjoyed each others' company, stumbling around like drunks in zero visibility, keeping busy and warm. But we were bushed and ready for our sleeping bags.

In the cave there was hardly any air movement. The door was open but below the platform; the colder air gravitated towards the tunnel, forming a dam for our warmer air, above. Diane rigged the candle that Rob had imagined, its faint light reflecting on the snow walls. We arranged the bags with the head-end farthest from the door at the higher end of the platform. Leaving only boots and parkas in the tunnel, we took our clothes into our bags, keeping them warm for the morning.

After the first few minutes needed to warm up a down bag it was very comfortable. Inside, it was as quiet as the snare-drum tent must have been deafening outside. It was just below freezing and there was no condensation dripping from the ceiling. Though tired, we were loathe to sleep. We wondered at our eerie cocoon-cave, wondered about Rob and Rick outside in the tent. Would the fresh snow hide the crevasses, making our ascent dangerous? Would our long drive be rewarded by our seeing the eclipse? We talked, probably over an hour, about mountains, people, life and living, till our wound-up brains ran down.

Mountain experiences start with the gross physical body challenging nature, then they progress to the emotional, to adventures of the spirit. While focused on the goal of a climb, the summit or a specific route, I am not distracted by meaning, but when forced to wait, the analogy of the mountain environment impresses itself upon me, makes me examine the process, the meaning of our efforts.

I realized the vital importance of my companions in the mountain trip, the learning that was available anywhere that I could take the time to examine any given situation. Dug into its surface, I felt the Mountain symbology of enduring strength and stability, accepted it as my own symbol of spirit. This cave was not the summit of Mount Hood, but it was, for me, the heart of this mountain. It was a secure shelter where awareness became particularly acute, a watershed for my understanding of the process of mountaineering and of life as a journey.

I woke several times in the night, mostly to readjust position, as my back was now giving me notice of several years' pain. I could hear the gentle whine of wind outside the tunnel; could feel a slight movement of cold fresh air on my face. Once, between sleep and wakefulness, I dreamed of seeing the tips of my skis, hearing their crunch, crunch, crunch, crossing an invisible wasteland through a dense mist. They followed a row of red tapes tied to bamboo wands, each one barely visible from the next one in the row, leading from nowhere to nowhere.

I had set my alarm-watch for 6:30 am, about half an hour before the eclipse time. I got to it on the second ring. Diane didn't even move. Slowly I realized where we were. It was still dark in the cave so I turned over to light the candle.

My shoulder grazed the ceiling. "What the hell?" I was aware that something was wrong. "Diane, wake up. The bloody roof is down at least a foot."

Immediately she sat up and bashed her head on the ceiling. In a panic situation Diane freaks even faster than I do. With a flashlight we could see our feet, and below the platform, the narrow entry way. But, it was almost impossible to turn over from one side to the other.

"Christ, we've got to get out of here!" Diane started wiggling her bag over the edge into the walkway-trough. We had to slither down the platform in our bags, retrieving gear as we went. We grabbed our boots and parkas in the tunnel and slid feet-first out into the day.

In the haze of drifting cloud, we looked at each other in disbelief, like skiers who have survived an avalanche and cannot quite believe that they are alive. Then the cold of the morning got us moving. We pulled on boots, shook the snow out of the bags and stowed them in our packs. The wind had dropped. The roar of the Primus came from inside the tent. Something was cooking. Diane stuck her head in and the rest of her followed. Rob was getting ready to feed oatmeal into a pot when someone pulled the shades! Cloud, or no cloud, this was clearly the eclipse. Shouting with glee, we stumbled out of the tent. Absolutely nothing to see out there. No sun, no half-sun, no place where the sun should have been, but wasn't! Though fog-bound, we were definitely in the umbra, elated by the darkness of the eclipse. Now I felt that the expedition had a focus, a *raison d'etre.*

After ten minutes the lights came back on. Abandoning our summit plans, we packed up and skied down to the Timberline Lodge, staying right under the T-bar line to avoid losing our way. It had been difficult skiing the day before. Now, carrying packs and having no horizon for reference, it was plain impossible. My back had gone rigid, becoming more painful with each of the many wipe-out; I could hardly take off my pack at the bottom.

Two days of fog, an overnight blizzard, the near-collapse of our snow cave, then the unseen eclipse--even without a summit attempt it had been an experience. Weather had set the theme, put me in touch with the mountain. In the mountains, weather is always an objective hazard, one I cannot influence, only adapt my plans to suit. But my attitude to that environment changes it from being a frightful enemy, to an acceptable, sometimes even an enjoyable companion.

Back in the city, my tasks will show success or failure by the way I approach them, whether they be in the office, in family relationships, or in a solo job of creation. Regrettably, in normal life or in the mountains, I have not always been proud of my actions. My challenge is to bank those experiences, to change the next situation! Depending upon experience and attitude, a blizzard (or my whole life) can be a fearful cycle of events, or a thing of joy, power and excitement.

Mountaineers try many strategies for their return to civilization: beer stops in taverns that have barely recovered from the previous night's fights, milkshakes to rebalance the body's electrolyte, big feasts at the salad bar diners along Highway I-5. We used them all. Rob dug out the soggy copy of "Fifth Business" and read with glee. Rick drove. Diane and I read our chapters in turn. But we weren't into the expression like Rob, or like we had been on the drive down to Mount Hood. With every pause, conversation would go back to the snow cave. And Rick would have another attack of claustrophobia, nearly driving the van into the median.

"If that drift had collapsed, you guys would never have got out! We wouldn't have known till morning." He shuddered as though he was back in there himself...

"I just slept like a log," Diane said absently, "never woke up, never even dreamed."

But I had. And before we left our camp, I had examined the roof over our shelter which nearly had become our tomb. And there had been fresh ski tracks, right over the cave, past the tent, just as though they were following a row of red tapes tied to bamboo wands, leading from nowhere to nowhere.

--oo--

On Mount Hood, time had been a factor for introspection, for intuitive learning from emotions. I had a chance to separate myself from daily and business worries, to experience something I had increasingly come to define as "soul." The soul is individual; its nature is self-defined. I needed time away to find it. For some, aloneness is achieved very quickly, even in a crowd. But I needed time.

Even the words are similar--soul and solo--the one evokes the other. Going solo is one way you can find it. My first attempt at going solo was a loop around Mount Temple from the Valley of the Ten Peaks. I was just out of university, living in Calgary at the time, a complete greenhorn with no feel for the dangers of mountain walking, none of the techniques for travelling safely in the hills, only a spiritual longing to be among the peaks, to experience the body-mind exhilaration of a day of moving from valley to ridge to valley.

Leaving my car at Moraine Lake, I had hiked up the well-worn trail to the plateau, threaded my way through the streams and larch woodlands to the cirque below Sentinel Pass. Above, the switchbacks were visible in the snow and I climbed them, one by one, feeling the isolation, the undefinable lifting of the spirit in the presence of steep rock and ice glistening in the summer sun. At the pass two climbers crashed towards me down the scree from Temple, their mysterious slings and hardware jangling about them. Their route, they said, was "just a grandmother's walk."

“Some grandmother that would climb Temple,” I thought as I descended down the other side of the pass. I remembered news reports of several climbers dying on the mountain; a well-organized group had lost several members in an avalanche.

I hurried down the large slippery boulders into Paradise Valley. All around the Horseshoe Glacier were incredible peaks: Hungabee on the left, then Lefroy and Aberdeen, with the snow tongue leading up to The Mitre, poised between them. Two dots near the summit of that steep snow climb moved like snails. They were mountaineers nearing the pass that could carry them over to the Lefroy Glacier and down. The peaks were active with that heroic breed--mountain climbers!

Paradise Valley had echoed with the roar of a mountain spring day. Pausing at Lake Annette I had skipped rocks across the still-frozen skim of ice, listening to the hollow, eerie echo of the stones bouncing on the lake’s sounding board. Then, on down the trail to the Moraine Lake road.

Hiking solo stimulated my imagination and intensified my bond with the peaks. These early hikes had a profound effect on my impressionable psyche, a vacuum needing to be filled. As a teenager I had always been interested in athletics, but disliked team sports. Introverted and physically small, I felt intimidated by many of my fellows. In track events, especially endurance races, I could hold my own. But hiking and climbing gave vent to my need to excel in something--anything! Successive trips drew me in deeper. Imagination was the only limit to adventure, till I realized that going solo meant getting back solo, too. There were some adventures for which I needed a companion.

The next task was to learn how to avoid bragging about my exploits. With a tentative approach to social or sporting situations, it was impossible not to talk about something I could do well. My brother, Ken, gave me the best advice:

"Keep it to yourself. A secret, once told, totally loses its power. And if someone finds out, it is worth much more than if you tell them." Little did I know, then, that this is a precept of the Tantric chants, where the monks avoid learning the meaning of a chants, so as to discover the mystery and power themselves. (For me, the aggravating Buddhist method of teaching.) Would I have given more credence to the teaching, knowing it came from an ancient monk instead of my brother?

Everyone depends, to some extent, upon the approval of others. Yoga taught me psychological independence, reliance on valid, self-motivated ideals, in an atmosphere of self-acceptance. If I am doing a sport or some other action I have chosen, not one determined by others, then there is really no need to publicise it. Climbing, because of the effort and risk involved, encouraged me to be clear about the physical and emotional tasks I was shouldering. And the mountains provided their own rewards, right at the beginning.

Going solo in nature can create a myriad of impressions: inspiration to adventure for the young, self-assessment for those who are open to learning, and memories, even nostalgia, for the old. It is the latter now, that recalls our honeymoon visit to Moraine Lake, the canoe gliding across the crystal lake to the foot of the Wenkchemna Glacier under the shadow of the Ten Peaks. On our hike up Babel Creek to Consolation Lakes, Jean had led on the trail through the tall conifers, striding out to keep warm in the September morning. Reaching the lake at the end of the trail, we perched on a huge block of rock under the icy cliffs of Mount Fay, and wondered at why anyone would call so beautiful a place only a consolation. For what could have been expected if this was the consolation?

Many years later, this time with some of the knowledge and the equipment of mountaineering, I returned from the west coast to Moraine Lake. Once again I started up the switchback trail to the Larch Valley. At the first corner was a notice board with the usual cautionary notes about bears, garbage, camp permits. Another notice hung from the sign's border. Scrawled in ball-point pen, it was an appeal from someone for help in finding a camera.

"My boyfriend was killed recently on Deltaform Mountain. If anyone has found his camera, I would appreciate recovering a record of the last hours of his life."

All the way up the trail I wondered about the young man and the accident. Had he been pressing too hard for the summit, or was he simply a victim of Deltaform's notorious loose rock? Had he thought about why he climbed, about how his risk-taking might affect others?

With such sobering ideas to distract me the switchback effort was nothing and within two hours I was camped just below the steep face of the Sentinel Pass cirque. Surprisingly, the Ranger at Lake Louise had given me a camp permit for the upper Larch region, probably because I guaranteed I would burn no wood. In the twilight of the late summer evening, I blessed the Ranger who had been so accommodating; blessed all creation for making me the only man camped here and not the one on Deltaform.

The dawn found me already climbing above Sentinel Pass. By full light, I was just beneath a pillar for which the Pass was probably named. Swinging to the right below a cliff band, I followed an old trail of footprints up several steep snow patches onto a ridge of alternating slab sections and pockets of scree. There was no technical difficulty, but I was glad of my iceaxe and the psychological comfort it provided.

The rising sun lit the Ten Peaks range across the valley, an irregular wall of snow, ice and rock stretching the entire length of Moraine Lake and beyond. Mount Fay snowfield, unseen from the valley, covered the north end of the range. Somewhere up there were two mountain huts, the Fay Hut on the south side of the range and the Graham Cooper Hut above the steep snow couloir between Peaks 3 and 4. Across my whole southern horizon, peaks of awesome beauty and horror ranged, even around to the most westerly, which was Deltaform. I was headed that way, not to that mountain, but to Wenkchemna Pass below it.

As I turned back to the ridge I noticed below the cliffband a small group of climbers moving towards me. With the renewed confidence that someone else thought that this was the correct route and with the determination to be the first to the summit that day, I kept steadily at the slope, glancing first east to the widening expanse of the Fay Glacier, then west to the peak of Lefroy dropping steadily below me.

Finally, I reached the summit on a wide snow field. Temple is the highest peak in the Lake Louise region, the first peak over 11,000 feet in the Canadian Rockies to be climbed. That 1894 climb was made by three Americans who must also have stood enthralled by the white expanse of the Sleeping Beauty Range and the green swath of the Bow River Valley. The Trans Canada Highway and the ski runs opposite on Mount Whitehorn, slashes cut through the coniferous forest, would not have been here, then.

Leaving the summit I met the group which had been following me. They were four Japanese climbers. In limited English they explained that they had come to Canada only two days before, were planning some climbs near the Columbia Icefields and that Temple was a warm-up climb. Not knowing the route, they were pleased to have me to follow! We exchanged photographic favours. They were snapping a panorama as I turned to descend.

Once off the summit ridge, I followed a descending snowfield left of my ascent route. Patches of white led nearly continuously down the mountain, through a gap in the cliff band to the heather meadow just above my camp. Although parts of the route were hidden from view, it looked steep but safe, a glissading dream for any mountaineer. My boot heels dug in nicely to control the speed; the spike of my ice axe gave additional braking and a third point of support. It was almost as good as skiing, but without all the necessary equipment. With a little down-climbing at the rock band, the whole descent to camp took under two hours, compared to over four hours to climb.

Waiting for the chilli to boil, I cooled my bare feet in a trickle off the snow. By the time the four Japanese had descended to Sentinel Pass, I was packed up and moving. The next hike was longer than expected. Short-cuts often are more work than the normal trail; the rib between the Larch Valley and Wenkchemna Pass was tiring with a full pack. The descent to the valley bottom was a succession of slippery boulders, dense and spiked scrub fir and, near the bottom, flowing grass and slippery slide alder. But once down to the deserted trail I bombed along to the edge of the snow, under the shadow of Deltaform.

It had been a long day already and the snowfield ascent to Wenkchemna Pass was a grind. The scene before me was rather daunting. Black clouds were hurrying over Mount Biddle, funnelling through Opabin Pass into this, the Prospectors' Valley. Contrasting with the clear sunlight of the morning, clouds had moved in and the temperature dropped, all unnoticed while I grunted up to the pass. Moreover, the slope from the pass dropped steeply for 300 metres before levelling out in the bottom. I recognized two rock-stacks, the Eagle Eyries, standing above the green of the valley floor.

A night in a storm on Wenkchemna Pass would not be pleasant. There was nothing to do but to get down as quickly as possible. By now, totally beat from the climb on Temple and the rough traverse to Wenkchemna, I jolted down the steep scree, using my axe to brake. The rain started. In wet grass and knee-height shrubs I charged on down, forgetting my aches in a race to get under cover. At the first little stream I found a flat spot, stuck up my tent and threw everything inside just as the sprinkles turned to splatters.

The lightning fired off the peaks from Biddle around to Deltaform, with no lag time between flash and thunder. The blinding light and deafening sound were almost coincidental. And with it, sheets of rain came, hammering the tent, forcing water through the seams. There was to be no cooking that night! I ate only dried fruit and nuts, washed down with water from my canteen.

Alone, I was acutely aware of my fear. Rationally, it was unlikely that I would sustain a direct hit, with high peaks all around. There was not a thing I could do about it, anyway. So I stretched my sleeping bag down the middle of the tent and stacked the pack away from the walls. Fatigue was winning. I lay listening to the barrage outside. But only for a few minutes.

The morning showed little evidence of the storm. Apart from steam rising from the heather in the slanting rays of sunrise, nothing indicated the evening storm's power. Nature delivers and absorbs, then moves on. It was another glorious summer morning. Lazily at first, I wandered past the Eagle Eyries, saw no eagles, but was nevertheless enchanted by their precarious balance and erratic, isolated location. Approaching Opabin Pass, the heat of morning, trapped between the steep cliffs of Biddle and Hungabee, made me strip down to a sweatshirt. But the snow field led up to glacial ice and I needed to fix crampons to get traction over the bare and slippery surface.

This was a rest day. At least, I planned no mountain summits. After threading the narrow pass, I got off the ice onto the scree where I removed crampons. By noon I had descended the Opabin Plateau and started across the ledges.

My sons, Ross and Glen, had hiked up to here when I was the custodian of the Elizabeth Parker hut for the Alpine Club. The whole family had been there and together we hiked throughout the Lake O'Hara basin. Ross got interested in crystals. Climbers told him there were some above the ledges on Yukness Peak so we traversed them, eyes searching the cliff above us all the way to Lake Oesa, then across another high trail to the Wiwaxy Col. No crystals. But the focus of our minds was on crystals and the immensity of our surroundings, not on how far we had gone, or how high we had to climb.

That is one of the difficulties of going solo. The work is harder; the extremes of weather--even emergencies--must be dealt with alone. The mind is less easily distracted from the pain. But going solo lets me define my goal and methods, places the responsibility on me alone for safety and for completing, or aborting, the task. Yoga practice, most of which is done alone, had helped to reinforce this lesson.

Yoga *is* discipline, but not an externally applied regime. It is the use of thought to control the "ideas in the mind." Instead of allowing oneself to daydream or be influenced by a myriad of external influences, the yoga aspirant decides his or her philosophy and directs all thought patterns to that end. The disciplines, both the physical work of Hatha and the mental concentration required for meditation and other exercises, forced me to take responsibility for all my actions, not pass the blame elsewhere for my errors or lack of action.

But going solo also intensifies the pleasure, like the "here and now" of the Yukness ledges that morning. By two o'clock the ledges were behind me and I sweated up the last few metres to the rocks at Lake Oesa, dropping my pack where I could watch the other trail.

In less than ten minutes, Rick arrived! He had driven in from the coast solely to join me in an attempt on Mount

Lefroy. We had planned to combine for the climb and discussed a meeting place and time. I hardly expected it would all work out, but here we were. After a brief rest we faced up to the distasteful part of the climb, a 640 metre rise up a scree slope leading to the Abbot Pass hut. It lived up to its reputation. Admittedly safer than the other approach to Abbot Pass, which traverses beneath our notorious "mousetrap," the Oesa side shows a million years' evidence of erosion, of fine rock scree that moves every time you step. Two steps up, one slide back. Near the lake, the slope was gentle; the higher we climbed, the steeper and less consolidated it became.

Below us, several hundred metres behind, two climbers followed. As we sweated and stumbled upward, the two gained on us. Their packs appeared at least as voluminous as ours, yet their footing was better and they were moving smoothly and steadily.

Rick noticed it first. "You know, Gil, I think those two are women!" As he was unattached and with younger hormones, he was bound to notice. We had a dilemma. Now, should we climb harder and get to Abbot first, or slow right down?

Deciding to keep on climbing about as fast as the heat and the scree would permit, we arrived at the hut at the same time as blonde Janine and raven-haired Maria. They did not mention our tardiness on the slope. And when they discovered that we hoped to attempt Lefroy in the morning, Maria made much of such virility and offered us wine from the bottle she had packed up to the pass! All this, along with flamboyant earrings and manicured fingernails, was rather hard to picture in a mountain hut. It certainly was a different arrival from my first visit here, en route to Mount Victoria.

The situation held certain potential for Rick. Janine was an entertainer at one of the clubs in Lake Louise and

Maria worked as a cook there every summer. After two months of weekly climbs their fitness was not surprising. About the time we were finishing the wine another hiker arrived up the snow route from Lake Louise. Mustached, handsome and glib, this young schoolteacher from Terrace quickly outdistanced Rick. So, while he romanced the blonde Rick and I hiked up toward the snow slope at the base of Lefroy, examining the routes to tomorrow's more accessible objective.

We left at first light. Lefroy is not a particularly long climb. Only 530 metres above the Pass, it is nevertheless a fickle mountain, claiming more than the usual number of casualties. This is because the mountain is rather accessible or, perhaps, that it consists of a series of steep ice routes, the condition of which is variable and unpredictable. (The first casualty was P. S. Abbot in 1896, who fell to his death while climbing unroped, and thus unintentionally became known to all who later used the Abbot hut.)

Rick led, not to impress anyone else still at the hut, but by prior agreement with me. The first two hundred metres of the climb was straightforward and we were able to kick steps in the snow. As the slope steepened, we attached crampons and continued up, aware that the snow was becoming shallow over the ice and that the steep face was getting closer to our outstretched hands. Rick angled over to the rock rib, right of the ice runway. I passed him all of my ice screws. Placing one for protection, he climbed while I belayed. Ignoring the long slide below us if we should come off, Rick climbed steadily and confidently, placing a screw periodically for a running belay. Soon we were moving together again. Eventually the slope began to round off; the snow depth increased, permitting easier step-kicking to the summit ridge.

A few delicate moves were required to traverse the rock ridge to the actual summit block. Even more hazardous was the hasty scrambling needed to achieve a summit photo with both of us in it, taken by timed shutter on my camera from an adjacent block.

The descent was frightening. For most of our route we faced outward for better mobility and balance, but the angle of the snow was near the limit. Just keeping the crampon points jammed into the surface required constant care. On the steep section we tried the rock rib, found it more difficult, reverted to the ice and finally bypassed the crux. The steepness eased. A half hour on the lower slopes brought us safely down to the hut. No one was there.

We packed up our overnight gear and started the long dusty slide down the scree to Lake Oesa. All the way down that horrible scree, then descending the trail to O'Hara, Rick and I commiserated on the relative merits of youth, beauty and adventure, and how our access to two of these seemed to be diminishing. We could still find adventure.

--oo—

While it was still spring when I left Canada, summer was already firmly established in Greece. I was alone, this time on the path that led up to the ridge, perhaps 300 metres above. As the afternoon wore on the sun grew steadily less oppressive and I was able to enjoy climbing slowly up the switch backs through the heather and nodding yellow daisies.

This was not wilderness like in Canada. Occasionally, I stumbled on a partly buried pipe that paralleled the path, perhaps a rudimentary water supply for the village. I could turn and gaze across valleys of olive groves, see a winding aqueduct contouring the hillside, count the tour buses parked in a row in front of the gate to the ruins of Delphi.

I was in Greece, partly as a holiday after completing a consulting job in the Persian Gulf. I had established a solar heating firm in Canada a few years before. This led to several design commissions in Canada and for Canadian companies working abroad. Solar was, of course, a natural technology for a country nearer the equator, but our negotiations with a Dubai sheik had gone nowhere. My assessment was that the Canadians wanted too much for their technology. As technical consultant I had to explain the various options for manufacturing solar collectors and systems. It wasn't my problem if a deal wasn't made.

I had stopped in Athens to complete the technical report of the trip. I wanted it finished prior to landing into the confusion of a family and a business neglected for a month. I worked continuously, stopping only to duck out to the avenue for a Greek salad. The draft was soon completed and with three days left on my stopover ticket, I planned a loop trip through Delphi and Southern Greece. Mount Parnassus was just north of Delphi; they were intimately connected in legend and history. I had brought no climbing equipment, but doubted that any would be needed; it was only 2460 metres high and the oppressive summer heat must already have reduced the snow pack.

All morning the derelict bus had trundled along the highway from Athens. The noisy locals had been my focus, distracting my attention from the narrow roadways and careening traffic. At a bus stop kiosk, tacked above the cigarette display, was a huge poster of Mount Assiniboine of the Canadian Rockies! Some Greek must have been dreaming about my country's mountains while I was a pilgrim, of sorts, to his peaks. Finally, the bus had rattled into the town of Delphi. I found a minuscule room in the attic of a private home run by a tanned and weathered woman. The price was right.

My path was now a wagon road. The trail was one vehicle wide and definitely not for fast travel. Indeed, it recalled to me pictures of Greek soldiers, with their calf-length stockings, breeches and tasselled tams, man-handling artillery pieces over these passes, creating unexpected resistance to the invaders of this and other centuries. I rested on a rock, looking down to the ruins and the tourists teeming like ants in the pathways. Above me, a herd of goats crossed the pass from the other side and, pausing to gauge whatever threat I posed, skittered on down the road I had climbed. They were followed by a young boy with long dark hair, cord trousers and no shirt, carrying a stick which he waved to me as he dashed on down. Wiping sweat from my eyes I regained the path, now nearing the ridge.

The Parnassus of my dreams was not so much a mountain as a place in history. It was a fascinating region, once considered the seat of all wisdom, of fortune telling from the entrails of chickens, of words of the Gods from cloudy summits and spring fed fountains. Years before I had climbed its namesake at the head of Fryatt Creek in the Canadian Rockies. It was one of my first serious rock climbs; memories of vertical cracks and intricate ledge traverses heightened my longing for the original Parnassus.

None of this prepared me for the sight that leaped at me over the ridge top. The mountain appeared above a floating bank of clouds: pyramidal, snowbound and immense. In such a civilized country, Greek mountains should be less of an undertaking; the long, hot summer days should have melted the snowfields; the summit should have been nearer to Delphi. This was not a running-shoe, one day summit. There was no way that I could cross the intervening valleys and arrange equipment to mount a serious attempt in my remaining two days. My objective had been Parnassus and I had come with the intent, however poorly planned, of climbing it.

I remembered Chogyam Trungpa's book, *Cutting Through Spiritual Materialism*, discussing it with Doug Scott on one of his trips to Canada. *"Disappointment is the best chariot to use on the path of the dharma,"* Trungpa had written. To learn *dharma,* moral uprightness, I had to adjust my attitude. My research was inadequate and frustration was the result. Intellectually, I realized that it was better to use this opportunity to explore Delphi's ruins, waiting below. Emotionally, the loss of my goal was harder to accept.

The cliff I had avoided on my ascent now gave me an unobstructed view down into the ruins of ancient Delphi, the remains of the central temple surrounded by the treasury building of each city state, the amphitheatre contoured into the base of the cliff and the stadium stretching to the west among the red-bark firs. Slowly, I realized that the pull of Parnassus had brought me to a very special place.

Further to the west, modern Delphi clung to the slope, her coloured tile roofs and roadways set off by the white-washed stone and stucco walls. And behind me, watching over the scene--impersonal, lofty and remote, but most of all, enduring--was Parnassus.

I realized that my mood had changed entirely. The effort of the climb on such a hot afternoon, the myriad views and their historical context in the evolution of our own society was overwhelming. This was indeed a museum *in the round.* I was sitting in a place of history and could feel the presence of the souls of the past, perhaps even their wisdom. My disappointment at not having a chance to climb was now gone; my pervasive mood was of elation, of delight at being in that place near sundown.

Long shadows streaked the olive groves. Parnassus now was lost in cloud, save the lower snow slopes which caught the sun in a mantle of brilliance. Far below me the ant-like tourists were gone. The last departing bus, revving its diesel to climb out of the valley, roused me. Finally, I descended to the ruins.

In the stand of firs beyond the stadium the fence was constructed tight to the rock wall. Further down, there was a place where it had been broached before and I was up, over and inside, running along the red clay of the stadium floor in the body of an Athenian athlete. At the far end of the open-air oval, panting for breath, I became a part of that ancient competition. There were no human distractions to my experience of its history. A ring was formed by the bleachers, carved from Parnassus' stone, reminding me of how difficult it would have been to construct the stadium in the Greece of 400 B.C. In those times, their games and their wars were similar; how different they are today.

For years we had worked in the peace movement, trying to find ways that an individual could affect the deadly East-West confrontation. There were actions that were needed and we had to take them, whether the effect was obvious or not. But the work went on for so long; there was so little apparent success that burn-out became a major problem. About then, I had studied the Buddhist principle of non-attachment to things and ideas. If I could lose attachment to the success of our cause and rely more on what the Buddhists called "right action," I would not face disappointments, my investment would become the action, not the result. Successes may not be less frequent, but my attachment to results will be reduced! One brought up in the western tradition may never really achieve this dream of non-attachment. But during the dry periods of failure in political activism, of not reaching any objectives or goals, it helped to keep me sane. Indeed, I had developed a concept of "process living," that fit the Buddhist concept.

One year, with no apparent connection to the work we had been doing for peace (but perhaps the result of a "global brain" functioning in accordance with its many "cells") the East-West confrontation seemed suddenly to dissolve. The Greeks had experienced similar long periods of war, struggles to secure their northern borders, conflicts between Athens and Sparta, followed by peaceful interludes. Was it this peace which had fostered the cultural and philosophical advances, so much a part of western values of today?

Descending the steep switchbacks below the stadium, I stopped at the spring of Kerna, lodging a Canadian penny in the niche in the rock for luck. Then, in the open fir forest, I came upon the extensive rubble of the main site of the Temple of Apollo. Climbing up into the amphitheatre, I sat listening for the orator, wondering if Socrates ever had been to Delphi, wondering if their wars were any less fraught with anxiety for personal safety or for civilization than the wars of today. Did they, in their century, have to consider the differences between personal death on the one hand and the death of all civilization? Perhaps they thought of their wars as equally threatening, even as we are forced to consider global war today.

Below the stage were the cantilevered columns of the Temple, the roof beam long since having collapsed. The building outline was there, enough to suggest its former grandeur, but only the base and colonnade were intact. Along the road curving toward the valley were the remains of the treasuries that each city kept, from which to make their offerings, names from history: Sicyon, Thebes, Athens. Strangely, the Athenian treasure house was the only structure that was intact and complete. Had they donated more?

In the hurrying darkness, I descended the stone pavement past the Roman Agora, the market place stalls along the roadside. Near the entry was the base that once carried the bronze statue of the bull of Corfu.

Against this base leaned a small wooden ladder. It had been left on purpose, it seemed, to allowing late leavers to escape the wire confines gracefully, and I did.

"Climbing is a living metaphor for unifying one's existence. At its purest, climbing is done solely for its own sake, without anticipation of reward." *G. B. Schaller*

"Whom have we conquered? None but ourselves!"
George Mallory

My son Ross had reason to be excited, it was his first trip out of Canada. Flying in from Calcutta, he had spotted Everest--*Chomolungma* to the Nepalis--its pyramidal rock tower protruding from the north-east ranges, a long, white-whisper plume trailing off from the summit. We had flown halfway around the globe and soon would be in the alien land of Nepal.

It was strange enough for me. Every day we soaked up Kathmandu's teeming markets of jammed, open-front shops. We cycled to the Swayambunath Temple on the west hill, walked the full perimeter spinning the prayer wheels, then fed the monkeys on the parapet. On the east edge of town, we inspected the beautiful and quiet Tara Gaon hotel, designed to emulate each of the ethnic regions of Nepal. And in the evening, the screaming bats in the high chihara trees haunted our way back to our own hotel.

We were two of the Alpine Club's trekkers hoping to walk the loop around Annapurna massif. We all relished those two days--time to overcome jet lag and dietary upsets, days starting to feel the religious, cultural and economic differences from Canada.

Then, the dusty, bumpy ride across the western ridges toward Pokhara gave us a more intimate view of the mountain terrain. We careened along the precipitous switchbacks of the rocky road built for Nepal by the Chinese, past women sitting cross-legged using hammers to make yet more gravel from stones! We emptied the bus while it crawled over slides of spring avalanche debris. Finally, at our trailhead near the village of Dumre we off-loaded everything, dumping packs, tents and food supplies on the ground to be organized into porter loads.

Four days into the trek, I had misgivings. Ross was 16 years old, the youngest of the fifteen members of our group. I was responsible for him, concerned that he not disrupt the holiday trek for others. The rest were mature individuals--many doctors, engineers and other professionals. How would he fit in? How would he relate to them in their interests, in their appreciation of Nepalese culture? I doubted Ross' physical stamina. We had trained a bit before we left, climbing several lesser peaks on Vancouver Island, and walking the West Coast Trail along the Pacific Ocean in a hasty four days. Of course, we *had* done the tourist route on Mount Rainier. Rick and I took him up the usual route from Camp Muir. Afterwards, we agreed that Ross was out of it for the top 600 metres with a mild attack of mountain sickness. But he made the 4300 metre summit on his own. When we got back down below the upper icefield he became his normal self.

Here in Nepal he had developed a problem. Playing *frisbee* on irregular ground at our second night's camp, Ross turned his ankle. As I walked slowly along the trail, watching him limping ahead of me using the party's only iceaxe for a cane, I was concerned. Would he be able to get over the 5200 metre pass? It was only ten days ahead; I was afraid that just the two of us might be returning down this same route!

And I had a more subtle misgiving. What would Ross understand from this trip? (We had already learned how to wait, accepting that things didn't happen on western schedules.) Would he appreciate the way the Nepalese had adapted their subsistence agriculture to the harsh mountain environment, or their sense of community in the work each person did, from the very young to the very old? Would our three month saga put him farther behind his companions who had the continuity of school while we were wandering?

Of course, there are several kinds of learning. In my studies at the Yasodhara Ashram I was continually challenged by this new process of discovering truth. It was far different from my previous experience in learning. In school, at home, even in recreation we were told what to do. When later I attended university and entered business life, I made my own decisions, but still my conditioning ignored intuition. If you wanted to know how to do something, say, choose a career, you took a course, read a book, or asked a counsellor.

The Buddhist emphasis on self-understanding is much more rigorous. For the first time in my life I met people who knew the direction my curiosity was leading me, yet they avoided telling me of their experiences in those fields. If the student was told, they reasoned, he may feel that it was just someone else's experience that he imagined. If it was his own discovery, he could personally establish its validity.

I was impatient with this kind of teaching. Later, I learned that the subtleties of mountaineering follow the Buddhist mode. One can learn climbing techniques from another climber's instructions. But to understand the feelings, to integrate the spiritual, mental and physical aspects of the process, it is necessary to climb. The transplanted ideas of another alpinist do not suffice.

Ross wasn't worried about these subtleties; he was just experiencing a whole new scene. We trekked past the last of the lemon trees and poinsettia blossoms; we were already gaining altitude. The Marsyandi Valley had shrunk to a gorge, a defile where the sound of roaring water became almost oppressive. The wide rice fields were gone. Our trail meandered along the retaining walls of terraced fields, each about ten metres across, each with a clay curb and an inlet port for water. These were fed by level irrigation channels diverting water from the streams that knifed vertically down the steepening banks.

That night we watched two of our sherpa guides slaughter a goat they had led along the trail all day. They took forever to kill it; I wished they would put the beast out of its misery. I left, went to a grove by the river and sat in meditation, while Ross eagerly watched the whole gory procedure. When I returned, he laid out all of the details. Fortunately, everything from the carcass had been used and the delighted porters ran off to their camp with body parts we would have rejected.

Ross accepted these events better than I. Of course, I knew how the killing floors of our meat packing plants operated. Ours were just as brutal, but isolated from the ultimate consumer. Knowing this did little to ease the direct experience here. (Years later in a village in the Caucasus, I would see ceremonial killings of sheep as part of a religious festival. The blessing of the animal seemed to me to be less barbaric--a thanksgiving that we in the West seldom remember.)

In the days following, we rounded the bend of the river, heading west. Crossing the pass near Pisang we began to feel more at home. The valley was wider and higher, in a familiar coniferous forest. Ross' limp all but disappeared. We both took pride in covering the day's allotted distance at a spirited pace. Since we shared a tent, we always started out together, trying to beat the porters onto the trail. Each porter carried a load of about forty kilograms in a wicker basket suspended on his or her back by a leather tumpline; the whole load on this strap hung across the upper forehead. The men and women porters are amazingly happy and very tough. They carry loads for six hours a day, grinding up steep trails, often in poor weather, usually barefoot.

One day I tried lifting one of the baskets; after a

hundred staggering paces, I dropped it on a rock beside the trail, to the hoots of the porters! But we were starting to feel more a part of the culture. We spent many hours on the trail, stringing together phrases in the Nepalese language. We learned several simple, lilting songs; in the evening we taped the songs of the porters, then played them back, much to their delight.

Ross became accepted by the older climbers and they seemed to enjoy his company. He would often walk with them, or with his favourite sherpa, Jigmy. While most of the adults realized the cultural and economic gulf that separated us from these happy and diligent people, Ross did not seem even to notice. Here, and later in the big, teeming Indian cities, he would strike up totally natural friendships with rickshaw drivers and street ruffians, taking chances that I, with all of my preconditioned reactions, was loathe to do.

I welcomed Ross' independence. It was his first real chance to develop as an adult. I wished that we could all relate to other cultures in his same natural way. I was pleased to let him discover such an amazing part of the world. Besides, it gave me the opportunity to do the same, often to walk alone. It was clear that I could learn from my own son.

One afternoon I arrived at the camping meadow early and, inspired by the incredible north face of Annapurna, I climbed 200 metres higher, to a promontory above the valley, marked by a cairn sprouting prayer flags. Across the river was the village of Manang, where we would stay two days to acclimatize. Down the valley, Manaslu rose in snow-clad majesty, an 8000 metre peak we had passed beneath, unseeing. I made several such sojourns, sitting outside some abandoned herder's hut, peering down at the little villages and their squared-off barley fields with fences of piled stones guarding against the goats.

I wondered at the Nepalese name, Annapurna, "Giver

of Life." Surely it was not in physical terms, in fact, it contributed to the sterile climate of the region. It was simply their mystical God-symbol.

"What kind of a life would I live if I had been born here?" I dreamed. "What if I knew only my near neighbours, knew only subsistence farming, working every day except for the festival days when we would sing, dance and drink *chang*? Would I now be bothered by a lack of self-confidence, by relationships that seldom run smoothly or by continually wondering about what to *do* with my life?"

The average Nepalese seems happier that most Canadians despite his shorter lifespan. Could it be that the simplicity of working for survival, of a religion that takes its answers from nature, or indeed, their free and open social system might have created in me a different personality? As I descended from these high-altitude quests, I looked across to the ranges beyond the valley, knowing that I would still have become a climber!

In Manang, we camped on roof-tops, flat, mud-on-poles areas which were great for tents. The houses were usually two storeys high, the lower floor for goats and other animals, the upper one for the family. Each extended family lived in one big room and the cooking and heating was all done by an open fire. Often there was no chimney, so the smoke filtered out under the eaves. One house blended into another on the hillside; the stacked appearance looked like a futuristic townhouse project of a modern city. The villages always faced south, with windows and courtyards arranged to catch the sun. The townspeople wore woven caps and colourful shawls; their happy chatter permeated the little stores, crammed with essentials: soap, cookies, sugar, the ubiquitous plastic bottles, and *flip-flop* slippers for the rocky trails. In the evenings, pungent smells of cooking drifted up to our tents. It was an interesting place to be, but I preferred camping in the meadows. There were drawbacks to being on the roofs, especially for night toilet trips. I loathed defecating in the street or in someone's hay loft, notwithstanding the fact that everyone else did so. There was only one toilet in the town, three blocks distant. It was disgustingly filthy, poised strategically at the top of a stream bank.

That night it snowed and the wind came in hard from the west. We kept our tent upright by piling stones on the guy ropes. About 2 am, our nearest neighbor, Betty, crawled into our tent dragging a wet sleeping bag behind her. By the morning most of the tents were collapsed.

On our second day in Manang, five of us left at dawn hoping to reach Tilicho Lake, at nearly 5000 metres one of the highest lakes in the world. In 1950, Maurice Herzog had led a French expedition up the Kali Gandaki gorge trying be first to climb an 8,000 metre peak. Dhaulagiri and Annapurna both qualified; both could be reached from the gorge. He had come over to Manang alone, trying to find an easier route up Annapurna's north ridge and seeking food from the region. There was none available in Manang and, with nothing to eat, he had climbed back up to the lake, over the pass and down the west side to the Kali Gandaki.

Retracing Herzog's route, we climbed up a well-used path in the upper Marsyandi gorge in the early morning half-light. Passing a small village, we decided to travel along the ridge so the view would be better and the route-finding more certain. We started up the stream, skirting several gravel bars and periodically climbing over truncated ridges when the stream blocked our route. This was tiring and unproductive so I scaled the bank. Mac and the others still hoped for an easy route along the bottom and soon we were separated. Our shouted directions, up and down, were lost in the roar of the water. I was now alone, so I sat, waiting, wondering why I was carrying our only rope.

My reverie was disturbed by six yaks plummeting down the slope toward me. I got behind some large boulders and held the iceaxe at the ready. They came to an abrupt halt about ten metres distant and examined me as carefully as their acute noses and dim vision permitted. "They're just curious," I thought, as I edged out from the boulders and, glancing nervously at the pawing yaks, climbed slowly up the grassy ridge. No shepherd was evident, but the yaks stayed where they were, and soon I was well out of their purview.

Determined to prove my route the best, I climbed as fast as I could, in a direct line towards the black pinnacle to the north of the col. I judged the lake to be between me and the saddle, so all I had to do was to head straight along the ridge to reach the lake. Now on hard snow I made good time despite the noticeable lack of oxygen. I was at 4500 metres. Even in the bright sun it was barely above freezing. The long morning was starting to wear on me and I stopped for a snack. There was no sign of my companions. I gave them up to the valley bottom.

Squatting, I noticed tracks in the snow that appeared to be from wild sheep--no one would graze goats so high.
I tried to recall details from Peter Mathieson's book, *The Snow Leopard*, in which he searched for the blue sheep and the almost extinct white leopard. His had been a mystic journey through Nepal, far west of where we now trekked. I often experienced many of the same day dreams as Mathieson. The isolation, the altitude contributed to an "other worldliness," both strange and uplifting, as I wandered solo, far beyond any settlement. There was a gradual reduction in my mental background noise. My physical effort was part of the reason, but more important was the lack of human stimulus. I found that, without this distraction the mind goes on a holiday, chews over everything that is current, then sorts it all and files it away. The result is a greater focus on the task at hand, an increased awareness and blending with surroundings, yet also a heightened creativity of thought. A bit like meditation.

So, in a mood much less determined, but still keen to see beyond the next hump, I continued upward. On my left, one ridge over, was Herzog's Grande Barriere, the endless snow wall defending the north side of Annapurna. To my right, I could see up to the pass, the Thorong La, that we were to cross two days later. For another two hours I pushed westward toward the black pinnacle which seemed never to get any closer. Finally, I reached a point at which I had to turn around.

I sat on my pack in the snow, looking west to where Tilicho Lake surely must have been. I was easily as high as the lake. But, realistically, it was still three hours away. Now I really wanted to get there, to see over the pass that Herzog had crossed. But I had no tent, little food, only a down jacket and poncho. I would be miserable, cold and hungry. But, I could survive a night at the lake and return to Manang the next day. However, I had not told our leader, Mike Rojik, of that possibility. I had not even discussed it with Ross. If I did not return they probably would send a party looking, even if there was no need. The law in the mountains. I had not alerted them to a possible bivouac; it was up to me to try to get back.

The snow plume was blowing off Roche Noire high on the north end of Annapurna's ridge. In 1950, Herzog and Lachenal had struggled up past it on the Sickle Glacier en route to the summit. They climbed the first 8000 metre summit in extreme weather conditions, but froze hands and feet during the descent. Both were carried by porters down to the southern plains. They survived, but endured painful amputations and eventual recovery. In the climbing world, they were heroes.

To the south the Grande Barriere was already in shadow. I was as relaxed, heading down into the late afternoon, as in the morning I had been tense. Now, there was no sense of failure, of missing the goal so strongly in my mind that morning. It was a surreal dream, with me floating down the ridge, finally getting off the snow into the noisy, water zone. Life was reawakened, evidenced by birds, sheep shit, picas whistling, and water. Everywhere--sparkling, bouncing, singing water!

The sun was already below the tip of the black pinnacle behind me. I knew that the tropics held virtually no twilight. Yet I could not focus on speed. I sloshed down a sheep path, thinking that this was no way to construct a trail. "You have to divert the water off or it will erode."

So with maybe three hours of daylight left, still on the high ridge, I built several rock diversions and saved that part of the trail. This occupied a valuable hour. I started down again, only to find the stream collecting on the trail. Again I dragged rocks onto the path, built another slanting dam, and walked on, only to find the trail awash three hundred metres further down. It became almost a game. Despite the long descent still needed to reach Manang, I could laugh at myself, at my ridiculous priorities. I really wanted to stay up there.

In the face of exhaustion, or sometimes fear, the rational process is suspended. One often acts without the balance of a sane person. On the other hand, what is balance, what is sanity? Can we say, "After exhaustion, comes enlightenment?" I was totally at peace.

I found a direct route down off the ridge to a high camp of the herders. It had been vacated. Finally, I got my mind to concentrate on getting home. In the last rays of sun I plunged down into the valley. Exhausted, I stumbled into the village we had passed at 6 am that morning. "Have you seen the climbers? Four men? Did they go past?" My enquiries were understood.

"Yes, about two hours ago. Do you want to sleep here?"

"How long to Manang?"

"One hour, if you run."

I ran. But it was soon pitch dark and I had to slow down. In the conifers there was no sky light. The tropical shades had come down firmly. At last I crossed the bridge over the Marsyandi River. Above me I could just make out the piled rock walls by the trail, hear the noises of the village. Soon I was back at the tents on the mud rooftop, to the relief of Ross and the rest of our party. I was back at the camp, where an old man drums and chants to the gods every morning at four.

--oo—

The sherpas had worn out their welcome even with the girls in the houses below us. Lolling on the porch in the morning sun, they contributed nothing to the busy life of Manang village where everyone worked through the daylight hours.

But while they relaxed, we acclimatized, getting our bodies used to the altitude. Ross and I explored the ridges north of the village, neglecting only the south bank of the valley where long gullies of avalanche debris reached up to Annapurna's snows. Ross was getting stronger, denying my earlier worries. We had taken to wandering in the neighbouring towns along the Marsyandi River, especially the little monasteries, often perched on a promontory above the village.

In Braga temple, a special ceremony was proceeding when we poked in our heads. We quickly sat in a vacant corner. The chanting was led by an older man; six monks answered his prompts, accompanied by a lone drum and cymbals. After about thirty minutes the chant reached a climax of sound and speed, then faded to nothing. After a few minutes of silence the old man came to us carrying two spherical "candles." He offered to us a mixture of seeds from a bowl, indicating that we should eat. Before we left Kathmandu we had been told not to eat uncooked, unwashed food. By carefully following this advice we had avoided the "Himalayan Horror"--diarrhoea and intestinal infections. Ross remembered and refused the food. It seemed to me to be a time for an exception; it was like presentation of *prasad*, a gift that ended our evening prayers at the ashram in Canada. So, I accepted and saluted him with folded hands and the Tibetan prayer: *Om mane padme hum*, which means roughly, "See the perfection in the centre of the lotus flower." The lotus (*padma*) is the highest point of spiritual and psychic knowledge, symbolically located at the top of the head.

His weathered features cracked into a grin. Putting down the bowl he handed us a candle each. The round yellowish ball was topped by a splash of reddish wax. But there was no wick. Then, he broke the side off one ball and offered it also to be eaten. Its coarse, mealy surface resembled ground wheat. *Tsampa!* It was barley, partly cooked and topped with rancid, dyed butter. The flavour was bland, but it was very substantial food. Tsampa had earned a reputation for nutritional staying power. Back at the camp, we shared bits of tsampa with the other climbers, but in the end the porters got it and happily stowed the remainder for the trek over the pass.

Despite being in the tropics, these high-altitude passes were hazardous. We had met some Swiss hikers looping Annapurna in the opposite direction. Crossing the Thorong La they were caught in a blizzard. Two of their porters actually froze to death! When we heard, we were aghast. Mike was already prepared for such eventualities. On his instructions, we carried extra coats and footwear in our baggage for the porters. To prevent them from selling the equipment in the villages, we kept it for issue only on the final leg up to the pass. Now it was time.

As leader, Mike Rojik was respected by the sherpas

and porters alike. He had been coming to Nepal for years. He knew the language and had built schools in a valley he frequented. All the porters were picked by Mike and the Sirdar, who was his trusted companion. Leaving Manang, one of the porters who had been limping on the earlier segments had to give up, to return to his valley or Kathmandu for medical attention. In this part of Nepal, the only way to get to a mountain or a hospital was to walk. He reluctantly gave up his load to be shared around. Shaking hands all around, he came to Mike last. He burst into tears when Mike patted him on the shoulder, wished him a safe journey back.

Mike arranged for two porters to carry firewood. There would be none available where we were to camp for the night. Our entourage of 15 climbers, 6 sherpas, and 20 porters wound up the trail towards the Thorong La. Approaching 4200 metres elevation, even our Nepalis started to slow. We crossed beneath a long scree slope, which was continually rolling rocks down to the trail. Each porter's head was immobilized by the tumpline from his 40 kilogram basket. But eyes and ears were alert for bounding rocks. Again we heard their prayer: *Om mane padme hum.*

At this high meadow a cold night was expected. Each of our tents took in two porters. Immediately, we knew we did not want the extra coats back; they were imbued with the permanent aroma of the working Nepali. The rest piled into a pyramid tent and huddled in their thin blankets till the sun was high enough to touch the meadow.

Ross and I were nearly the last away in the morning but made steady progress up the ridge to the snowfields below the col. Here and there were bodies of cattle frozen in the blizzard and not yet scavenged by man or bird. We passed other climbers of our party, also porters struggling on snow with their new and unfamiliar shoes. The trail meandered 3 kilometres over the snow-covered moraine before rising to the final saddle.

Despite our rapid progress up from the meadow, or perhaps because of it, Ross was tired and headed down the west side with two climbers, Barry and Paul. Above the cairn I rested, peering southwest up through the fleeting mists to the summit of Khatung Kang. The spectacular snow peak had been prominent, even from my high perch south of Manang and from the ridge route to Tilicho Lake. Now I strained to see, but caught only glimpses of rock buttresses laced with snow gullies. One of them would surely lead to the upper snowfield, eventually accessing the final tower. I knew the effort that would be needed, knew also what the feeling would be like when I arrived. I would be torn between fear and elation of that remote, dangerous place. Imagining the final few steps up the ramp to the summit, I could feel a tingling in my skin, the happiness that overrides pain and fatigue. Even sitting here I could feel the welling tears.

But the col was already 5416 metres, the highest I had ever climbed. There was no possibility for me to get up the extra thousand metres, at least another four hours of climbing, on that day. The clouds persisted, blocking the view of the steep slopes above the pass. As I waited, glacier lethargy took hold; my resolve evaporated. Alpine Club group treks were not set up for personal expeditions; a bivouac high on the plateau was out of the question.

Still, I wanted to get as high as possible and to test my climbing endurance at that height. I headed up the easier north side. Altimeter in my shirt pocket, I booted up the snow as fast as I could, my heart rate over 150 beats per minute. After a full hour on this treadmill I had only reached the cliff base, less than a 200 metre vertical rise! Not bad at that altitude, yet it was obvious that one day would not make a dent in Khatung Kang's defences.

Why had I climbed above the pass, or for that matter, spent a whole day alone looking for Tilicho Lake? By this time, I thought I had internalised the yogic lesson of clarifying objectives. Consciously, I questioned who I was trying to satisfy--some picture I was trying to create for others, or for some other personal reason? I knew that some of my motivation was for Ross, the other climbers in our group, maybe I was even trying to impress Mike Rojik. Of course, the terrain was inspiring; the rarefied air seemed to draw me to increased physical effort. Finally, I convinced myself that it was my own agenda. Like the day searching for Tilicho, I had started out with an objective in mind--reaching the lake. On the way, I lost that goal because of the distance, the physical obstacle. While searching for the goal, I had become *one* with the process; the spiritual prize came after I abandoned the original objective.

Back at the pass, I was well behind the last climber (the porters were already over the col and far below.) Three hours down the rocky, steep and dusty trail I spotted the tents already pitched and welcoming. At that altitude, a thousand metres up and then down was a long day.

Muktinath was rather different from the Marsyandi side of the pass. As a religious mecca the town attracted Asian pilgrims and Caucasian long-haired tourists who followed the pilgrims, so that the whole valley had a commercial air to it, with well-stocked shops and salesmen hawking wares, and with restaurants selling *dahl, bhat, takari,* (lentils, rice, vegetables).

Even before my boots were off one seasoned Nepali woman descended on me with blankets, shawls and an array of Tibetan ornaments for sale. Not wishing to carry any more than I had to, I resisted her successive price cuts for a beautiful, multi-coloured, yak-hair blanket. Finally, the price was ridiculous, about twenty dollars; the blanket was mine. The aroma threatened to infect all of my other gear, but then, we had been on the trail two weeks ourselves. Immediately I fell in love with the blanket, lightweight and yet very warm.

On cool mornings I wound it around my shoulders like a Tibetan version of an Arabian sheik.

Down the dry, windy, Kali Gandaki river valley we hiked, past Jomosan with the bell-ringing donkey trains, past farmers guiding oxen pulling single-share wooden ploughs, past the airport where, occasionally, a Royal Nepalese Airlines plane (a Canadian Twin Otter) lands. The valley is so deep and the winds so erratic that they only fly during the morning calm.

High on our left were the peaks of Nilgiri with Annapurna behind, on the right the soaring east ridge of Dhaulagiri, the Nepalese "Mountain of Storms" a name very descriptive of the physical presence. Though one of the first 8000 metre peaks scouted by Herzog and other western climbers, Dhaulagiri was one of the last to be climbed (by Max Eiselin's 1960 Swiss expedition).

The Larjung campsite below Dhaulagiri was our home for two nights. The first morning, our "fearless five" from the Tilicho Lake trip, headed up towards the Dhaulagiri base camp. Resolving this time to stick together, we hiked up through rhododendron bushes three metres high. Some bemoaned our timing, the blossoms appearing only in early summer, but this fall visit at least allowed us to collect seeds. After a long, hot climb we reached the former base camp at elevation 4600 metres.

In 1969, seven climbers from the first American expedition were killed by an avalanche which wiped out their entire route only 700 metres above this base. After the calamity snuffed-out their attempt, this base camp was little used. But what a glorious outlook for a mountaineer's tomb! Between these massive ranges only 25 kilometres apart, the Kali Gandaki cuts through, a vertical relief of over 5400 metres from peak to river, one of the most dramatic chasms in the mountain world.

But to the south west, I was drawn towards a

beautiful snow pyramid. Maybe 2000 metres higher than our promontory, it looked entirely feasible, perhaps even for a solo climb. I was tempted to try this scheme out on our leader, perhaps to solicit a fellow-climber for a ropemate. But again, as with the Tilicho Lake trip and my sortie at the Thorong La pass, I was able to talk myself out of this danger/opportunity. Against the scheme were many plausible arguments: the schedule Mike had planned, the lack of specialized equipment for snow climbing, my responsibility for Ross who would remain in camp. More likely, the considerable effort and a fear of the unknown argued against such a scheme.

Then, why not discount such ideas as mere dreams? Why not be content to experience the trek itself, my companions, the Nepalese people? I seemed to be continually creating unique goals, ones that were unattainable in the circumstances. As a result a fear/ambition dichotomy arose that prevented a feeling of success in the process of mountaineering, perhaps also of living. Instead, I needed to concentrate on enjoying the events that were happening, not looking for something unique. Focused on summits, ego-oriented, I had been ignoring how little my own successes or failures really affected the essentials of life itself.

It snowed that night. Descending the next morning, the porters preferred to be barefoot or to use thongs, giving us advice how we should place our feet (shod only with Vibram-soled boots) so as not to slip on the snowy trails! Foregoing the wet tents in the continuing stormy weather, we stayed the night in a “hotel” in Kalo Pani, rather a different experience than the snow climb I had visualized.

Then, in one day we dropped 700 metres through the backbone of the Himalayas to Kabre, where we could see out to the plains. Leaving the group trek high on the east bank, Ross and I took the old trail along the river, finding lizards sunning on the rocks and exposed, airy passages along the rushing river. We were nearing the end of the trek. While 70 year old Alex rented a donkey to carry him directly to Pokhara, the rest of us crossed several ranges eastward. Mike wanted to visit a village school for which he had raised money in Canada. At our camp beneath the spectacular Machhapuchare ("fish tail" in Nepalese), an impromptu concert was staged in Mike's honour.

All around the southern hills evening fires showed settlements, hitherto unseen. One by one, families began arriving, answering this communication without telephones, coming from valleys away to join in the party. The northern sector was dark. This was the foreboding wall of the Himalayas, with Huinchuli and Machhapuchare guarding the entrance to the Annapurna Sanctuary. This was the entry for many mountain expeditions, but notably for the 1970 climb of the south face of Annapurna by Whillans and Haston. The first high-altitude face to be attempted by an Alpine style climb, it was to set the mode for the next decade of Himalayan ascents.

I felt a magnetic pull to see into the Sanctuary. But, this time I knew there was no time, that I would not return this way, that I was leaving these mountains, probably forever. And, I was content. It was practical thinking ruling over dreams. Two nights later in the Fish Tail Lodge in Pokhara, we saw the whole of our trek delineated across the horizon, Manaslu on the east, all of the Annapurnas, Machhapuchare and Dhaulagiri on the west.

There are so many spectacular peaks in the world, how can a climber ever hope to complete them all? In my beginning years, I pursued a list of summits popular among my friends, then gradually moved further afield to the Rockies, Cascades, Alaska and even other continents. The more I explored, the longer the list became. As Doug Scott had said, it was a problem that all climbers faced, regardless of their place in the fraternity.

Whether I seek more climbs, or ones of higher difficulty, sooner or later the climbs will end, yet the list will remain, unfinished. I can continue to yearn towards the high places, and if the weather, my companions and other circumstances are favourable, I can go for the summit, even make a real effort and take a measured risk to reach the goal. But I will know it is the going, it is the process within me, and not the summit that is important. This view of mountaineering as a journey begins to change my attitude to the need for summits.

If the tasks extend beyond any hope of completion, does this change my efforts? Perhaps I will pursue other paths, more suited to age, health and psyche. If I can see my life as part of a continuum, or my daily effort as a process rather than a success or failure in reaching a goal, then the confusion in my soul is diminished. I can pursue the Buddhists' idea of "right action" as opposed to a list of chosen goals. But, the concept has to be accepted, to become integrated emotionally, not just a rational conclusion.

The Indian beer on our table tore my thoughts away from Nepal. It was the beginning of our psychological recess, that time and space between expeditions, time to absorb the decadence of civilized comforts, time to forget the draw of unknown pathways.

Instead of thirty trekkers and Nepalis travelling together through a remote region, Ross and I now became only two, alone amongst the millions on the plains. In a jungle camp in south Nepal we searched out elephants, rhinoceros and crocodiles, with competent guides to orchestrate our meetings. Then, by bus to Lucknow in northern India. At one stop the bus drove off without us! Fortunately, someone noticed us sprinting along behind. We quickly realized that it was up to us to find our own way, to keep our baggage in sight and to supply the needs of daily life. On the train to Dehra Dun we began to feel at home in the culture, especially on arrival, in the arms of new friends who hosted us and opened other doors for us in Delhi, Vadodara and Calcutta.

While in Dehra Dun, we travelled one day to Rishikesh, a town of pilgrimage on the Ganges. Arriving, we were glad to exchange our raucous bus for a sedate horse taxi. Along the legendary Ganges River, so close to its Himalayan origins, many have established ashrams for worship and study. Nevertheless, the taxi driver knew them all--in half an hour we stood before the gates of the ashram of Swami Sivananda.

It was here that Swami Radha had been called by visions while still in Canada. She had been a German woman of culture and wealth, a professional dancer. Emigrating to Montreal she began to experience visions of an unusual looking man, a man who turned out to be the great Indian doctor and spiritual leader, Swami Sivananda. In unique circumstances, Sivananda gave her direct and individual tutelage. Within months she progressed through various stages of spiritual awakening, revoking material life in favour of spiritual study. And it was here that she made a life commitment to her teacher, who then sent her back to establish her own ashram in Canada.

During our visit, Sivananda's ashram was nearly deserted. Swami Chidananda, who led the ashram after Sivananda's death, was travelling elsewhere in India. We were ignored, taken to be among the "merely curious" and not true seekers. Touring the steep site, we found monuments to the founder--printed slogans of disarming simplicity that I had heard many times before.

"God is love!"

"Do it now!"

The entire place, with its ramshackle buildings and the usual filth of India, disappointed us. But the mausoleum of Swami Sivananda was impressive. Taking off our shoes at the polished marble entryway, we proceeded into the grand hall. The central bier dominated the interior, replete with white, grey and black marble and decorated with semi-precious stones. I walked up to the glass enclosure containing the body of the great man in his dying pose. Meditating for several moments on all the amazing occurrences of his life, I felt a connection and a relevance of his teachings that I had experienced in Canada.

Turning to leave, I heard someone shout. A small man was running toward us, waving and pointing at Ross. I turned, realized the problem immediately. Oh, God! Ross was carrying his running shoes in his hand (to avoid someone stealing them while we were inside.) We departed the mausoleum and the ashram in disgrace.

Our month-long sojourn in India was a time of learning for us both, a real chance for us to coexist as friends, not just as father and son. I had arranged several business meetings, opportunities to search out companies working in "renewable energy:" solar heating, wind power, and biomass (the use of methane, generated from human and animal waste) for cooking. These meetings took us to Bombay and Vadodara on the west coast, to Calcutta on the east, touching the incredible past and present of India.

Between business encounters, we visited many of the usual tourist meccas, but by ourselves and on the cheap. In the pink stone city of Jaipur, Ross befriended a young rickshaw driver. One night they insisted on going to a Hindi movie together. I had seen one, enough for my tastes. Experiencing my first serious bout of diarrhoea, I decided to stay in the hotel. Ross was back at ten o'clock allaying my concerns about this unfamiliar city scene. We left the next morning, using his friend's rickshaw to carry our bags to the train station.

We had hoped to travel to Darjeeling from Calcutta, but could not get the permit for the area due to some rather ill-defined national security reason. So we chose our next objective, Thakurgaon in Bangladesh. There, Rahima, our foster daughter, a fugitive orphan from the violent break-up of Pakistan, lived in a home for girls. Leaving the Calcutta train at Pailguri, we paced the station platform enquiring about local transport to Bangladesh. There was none. Moreover, we were advised that we had come illegally to Pailguri. A permit was needed here also. The war had been over for years; India and Bangladesh were not even protagonists, though India had used their army to stop the flow of Bengali refugees. Why was the border still being treated as a hostile zone?

No one knew. A police official took us into "custody." A local bus carried us about 10 kilometres to the east; we all got off. The official pointed south and said, "That's Bangladesh. Walk straight ahead about an hour and turn right onto a road. Down this road you will find a village with a railway station."

We were left alone with our baggage in the tropical noonday sun. Already it was over 30 degrees C. Fortunately, we had packsacks instead of suitcases, and Nepalese umbrellas for sun shelter. It was a long, hot walk.

Perhaps it is best to forget our arrival in the village, negotiating Bengali currency, *taka*, at half the exchange rate from an opportunistic official. Then we survived an extremely crowded train ride with a deranged fakir loudly berating all the passengers. In the press of the crowd unloading at the station, I lost my wallet to a thief. (Luckily, we had split our *taka* and Ross had that plus a few travellers' cheques in his money belt.) Eventually, we were able to wheedle a ride 30 kilometres over to Thakurgaon where eventually we found her.

Rahima was a beautiful smiling girl nine years old, with black hair and deep brown Bengali eyes. She was the tallest girl in the school. Despite the lack of a common language, there was an instant bond between us. She showed us the school compound, mostly small brick and timber buildings, their chicken coop and cow, and proudly displayed her printing (which her teacher told us was only second grade level.)

We were there for four days, the last one being Christmas. Of course, this was not a Muslim holiday, but the head teacher knew its significance in our culture and decorated the gates and building with paper streamers. We added balloons brought from Delhi. Ross sacrificed our frisbee to the forty-odd screaming little girls. One would throw it, then all would run after it, arriving en masse on top of it. It lasted twenty magical minutes.

Christmas dinner was two half-fried eggs. After, Rahima passed out candy from a bagful we had purchased in Calcutta. It was an unforgettable visit. Ross wept quite openly as we drove in the jeep out the gate and back to Saidpur to catch the flight to Dacca. The stopovers we had arranged--Bangkok, Hong Kong, Seoul, Tokyo, Hawaii, and Disneyland near Los Angeles--all were too long for me. I had already bridged my "psychological space" from the mountains, and from home.

--oo—

My troubles began at the Haridwar check point. All of the baggage thrown on top of the bus had cracked my plastic fuel jug and it was leaking kerosene down into the open windows below. Finally, I realized the cause of all the shouting, leaped to the roof of the bus and began to pitch the heavy sacks of potatoes off my gear which by now was on the bottom layer.

I grabbed the bottle and set it upright, hauled my pack away from the puddle. The guards seemed satisfied. As more luggage came aboard, I made sure that my pack went on top, but the damage had already been done. I climbed down and moved to the back seat inside, propping the leaking poly bottle between my boots. I opened all the windows near me, but the rank of kerosene pervaded, at least until several of the hillmen lit up their foul cigarettes. I pointed to the leaking bottle and made gestures to indicate the explosion of the bus. This did nothing but amuse them.

I muttered to myself, realizing that there was no one who would worry about the danger, no one to complain to, and most of all, no one who would understand how critical was my reduced supply of fuel.

But I had experienced this land. I was not new to India so I kept it to myself. It had been five years since my first trip with Ross. I was quite accustomed to being stared at, usually as the only Caucasian in the village. Certainly I was the only one on this bus. I was familiar with the pushing and shoving in the market, with the queues for railway tickets, with the persistent vendors on the city streets who simply took "No!" as a challenge.

It seems that Indians, long used to the press of humanity in such a limited land, had lost all consideration for their fellows. But I saw a paradox, because I knew that these same people were tolerant, sharing and were capable of unlimited patience. Consideration and patience did not necessarily go together.

I braced myself against the jolting wall of the bus and tried to soften the impact of the road on my weeping kerosene bottle. Already I was sorry I'd neglected my Hindi studies. On the bus were only hill people with little knowledge of English. We were climbing a meandering, one-lane road north from the Ganges River bound for Uttarkashi in the Garwhal Himalayas, still eight hours ahead.

I was on contract in India, designing solar systems and training young solar engineers for a Canadian-Indian joint venture company. By tenuous connection it was the result of my previous trip to Annapurna and the subcontinent. My current contract allowed some breaks and I wasn't needed in Delhi.

Only a month before I'd been home in Victoria (to look at the mail and pay the bills), then Jean came back with me for the next four month stint. We had both suffered from being apart, but the prognosis was for more of the same with me in Delhi and her working at the Dehra Doon hospital. Jean and I travelled together in relative comfort by train to Dehra Doon. Second class air-conditioned was definitely the way to go. For that short journey, we absorbed each other as we were swallowed by India.

Jean planned to work at the carehome for lepers and tuberculosis victims east of Dehra Doon. After our holiday with Mady, she would stay in the nurses' compound there. Mady, mother of my Canadian friend, Dilsher, met us at the station and took us into her life. We met everyone, toured the countryside, even up to the Mussoorie hill station. Mady lived in the middle of a social cyclone. She was originally Austrian and had outlived two husbands, a Sikh engineer who was Dilsher's father, and the English headmaster of the Doon School. Active in charities, environmental causes and culture, Mady was both representative and conscience of the intellectual life of Dehra Doon.

She dumped Dilsher's duffel bag of old climbing equipment on the verandah and invited me to help myself. The kerosene stove was heavy and awkward for packing, late '50s vintage. I suspected that Dilsher had taken it to Nanda Devi when, as a boy of 16, he had hiked with a small party into the Sanctuary. The Nanda Devi Sanctuary also had been my objective, but the area had been trampled by hikers since the days when Tilman first climbed the 7820 metre peak in 1937. Two months before I applied, the government had simply closed the area. I had to settle for the western part of Garwhal as an alternative.

The bus bumped to a stop at Tehri. Directly outside my window was a store whose primary decoration was a garland of polyethylene jugs draped on a cord around the doorway. It was only a ten minute stop, but it was long enough for me to buy two small containers, split the kerosene into them, find the least busy end of the main street for a pee (difficult, with three big-eyed urchins watching intently), buy half a dozen samosas from an open-front stall and hop back onto the bus as it was pulling up onto the grade.

By the time I reached Uttarkashi either the kerosene fumes or the spicy samosas had got to me. I was physically tired and psychologically worn from the dangerous driving above precipitous cliffs. And I'd had enough of bad cigarette smoke. So I quickly checked into the only obvious hotel and enquired as to the location of the Nehru School of Mountaineering. With my gear stowed behind a "sort-of" locked door and with the key in my pocket I was pleased to get out of town. Twenty minutes up the switchback road was a small group of buildings in a fir grove. Dilsher had given me some names of guides used by two previous Canadian expeditions. Mady had added a few more.

None of them were present. In fact, the school was deserted; the leaders had taken a new crop of trainees up to Harsil for a two week field trial. The man who met me in the lobby was a clerk, obvious from the ubiquitous, brown, vee-neck pullover that he wore. He knew none of the available guides in the village, could not tell me the standard rates of payment nor any of the essential data for hiring a guide. And no, the Director (who I had met at a Himalayan Club meeting in Delhi) was not in town and was not expected until next Saturday.

Back down the switchbacks I jogged and as I approached the hotel a black gorilla of a man stopped me.

"You wanted a guide?" He obviously had talked to the hotel manager.

"Well, I want to know what they charge." I answered. "Are you a guide yourself? Does anyone here know the western valleys?"

"Yes, I'm guide--from the School. But I can't go. My nephew--good climber, he go!" Frankly, this guy looked like the type that I wouldn't trust. Apart from being huge, with dark hair radiating skyward, he had a permanently furrowed brow. I guessed that it was acquired trying to keep his stories straight. Probably I was being unfair, but I was relieved that he wasn't available. But I still wanted to go to Sankre the next day, hopefully with someone who knew the area.

"I'm going to get some dinner now. If your nephew is available, I'll talk to him at the hotel in an hour." It was already dark, but I walked up the hill to the last house. There was the expected sign propped in the window, "Garwhal Guiding", but absolutely nothing in the building. A little boy followed me in. He could not understand my questions but with hand signs told me Mister Guide was gone to the mountains. So much for that guide. So much for the crampons I'd hoped to rent here. So much for any serious snow climbing.

Back at the hotel I had just finished a plate of brown lentils and potatoes cooked with incredible amounts of chilli when black "Bart" appeared with another man in tow. His nephew, Kulshan, was thankfully of a slighter build, about 25 years old and with a pleasant face. He smiled a lot, and soon I realized that this was a substitute for speaking English. He had been a student at the Nehru School and lived in Sukhi, 50 kilometres to the north. Bart and I agreed on a price which I wrote in my booklet and showed to Kulshan. He understood money. I had no idea what technical ability he possessed, but he had climbed Swargarohini (about 6,000 metres), a steep ice climb. He looked athletic. Small men (and women) always did well in the high mountains. Probably a more effective metabolism.

"You pay in advance?" asked Bart.

"Two day's pay when he gets on the bus with his climbing gear," I countered, "the rest when we get back to Sankri." That seemed good enough. Soon I was dead to the solid wood of my hotel bed, and dead to the raucous noise of the street below my window.

In the half-light of the dawn I found the bus to Sankri, humped my pack up onto the baggage rack, then settled in a window seat with the two poly jugs of kerosene, one now leaking, at my feet. The bus slowly filled, but nowhere was Kulshan. The driver revved up his engine and the ticket man started collecting the fares. He gave no tickets in return, but nobody seemed worried. Just as we were about to pull onto the road, Kulshan appeared, wearing a faded red down jacket and carrying a rather small pack. I paid his fare and gave him 80 rupees for two day's pay.

Kulshan immediately jumped off the bus and ran over to the smoking fire in front of the restaurant. There was Bart, palming the money. So that's how it works! The payoff, the intro fee.

About thirty minutes down the road I began to wonder about my guide. He had moved to a rear seat by the open window. At intervals, he would puke out the open window, then sit dejectedly, waiting for the next eruption. Considering the twisting road and the way the driver hurtled his machine around hairpin turns, it was not surprising. Every bus window has a diagonal strip of puke below it on the outside; some doesn't make it out the window. But, with my kerosene spreading a pool on the floor I could hardly complain, just accept, withdraw, endure.

Six hours later we bumped down the hill into Mori. By now Kulshan's face was a darker shade and we were communicating with hand signs and some basic phrases. He knew a few words of English. I needed a toilet, but, of course, there was none. Kulshan indicated the river bank. I escaped my entourage of children and staring adults and found a few scraggly bushes beside the river. "This is absolutely the wrong place," I thought. But it obviously had been used for that purpose by many people, and recently. No wonder that even the flowing water here is suspect.

By the time I returned, the driver had dumped off all the baggage and the bus was leaving town by the way it had entered. Apparently another would arrive for the remaining distance to Sankri. After three hours and many cups of *chai*, sweet tea boiled with the milk already in it, another bus did, indeed, arrive. There was no glass in the rear windows; clouds billowed up from the wheels directly into our gear, our hair and our eyes. We forgot about the leaking kerosene.

Finally, in the abrupt tropical twilight, we were there. On an unused porch in the village we cooked lentils and spread our sleeping bags, more for privacy than for warmth. But the next morning's mists were cool and penetrating. Kulshan went off to find a porter while I repacked everything. We were down to one kerosene bottle, the other having a split seam. We used some, then topped-up the stove tank, but one bottle would have to do. We would use wood, or dung, if we ran out.

We walked the first 11 kilometres to Taluka on a jeep grade that was little used. It was relatively flat, threading along the east bank of the Supin River through chir pine, spruce and cypress. Beyond Taluka I started to sense isolation, especially as Kulshan and the porter were not yet in sight. I lazed by the gently-flowing river an hour, then Kulshan trotted up to my meadow. The porter had quit. The load was too heavy, the pay too little. (The last trip here had been a rather lucrative venture for the Indian Army, with porters paid four days for what was only a two day carry.)

A compromise. Kulshan found a new draftee, who would carry the duffel bag--almost 30 kilograms of rope, food and incidentals. I would pay the porter three days for two day's work. It was only about five dollars per day, but I'd brought only limited funds along. All the rates were escalating. Kulshan would carry the stove and kerosene in his free hands and his personal gear in his pack. I would lug the rest. As we sweated up the 1400 metre rise to Osla, I was not a happy camper. Used to living at sea level and pushing 50 years old, I was carrying over 25 kilograms of supplies. Kulshan lived at 2000 metres and therefore was used to the altitude. He loped along with 15 kilograms and the kerosene.

The rough trail rose steeply along the sharp gorge. On the other bank logs had been piled, awaiting the spring flood to carry them to the mill, much the same system as used years ago in Canada. We puffed up through conifer stumps to the bush above, surprising ten huge grey langurs who scampered off and swung up into the cypress trees calling to each other. "How much different is the Yeti from these animals?" The Yeti, the enigmatic beast that populates only high altitude, or perhaps only the imagination of the local people, apparently had been sighted less than 100 kilometres from our valley.

The afternoon was hot and the pack straps cut deeper hour by hour. "Why," I thought, "is the first day always the hardest? Perhaps it's because I'm not in shape and none of the heavy food has been eaten yet." After eight hours on the trail we dumped our loads at a forestry hut below Osla. Despite our initial difficulties, we had covered a lot of ground.

In the cool of the next morning we climbed from the valley floor past Osla, the last village. Perched on the north bank to catch the winter sun, it appeared unspoiled by outside culture, but affluent in its own rural sense with overstuffed hay barns and numerous sheep herds. We lingered five hours en route, absorbing the mountain scenes. At one corner we could see the whole of our past route along the Supin River. Up the valley, a lone patch of firs, our first sight of the Harki Doon meadows, marked our campsite.

The viewpoint divided civilization from wilderness and, while beyond it there were thousands of sheep and a few shepherds, it was a zone of solitude and peace. Another two kilometres along the trail we found their camp surrounded by large boulders under which sheep and shepherds alike crowded to escape the weather. Grasslands stretched east a few kilometres, then nothing but rock, snow and ice ridges.

We paid off the porter, who jogged on down the trail. By my bet he would be home before dark. After the crush of humanity in India I felt rather alone in Harki Doon. Kulshan spoke little, perhaps because we lacked a familiar language, but he seemed happy simply to point out the special peaks that he knew, then to find a few sticks of firewood and to prop and dry his boots in the fading warmth of the sun.

I didn't have the same sense of adventure, of a clear plan, that I had felt in previous expeditions. Having no one to share the effort or the scenery took something from the experience--there was too much uncertainty, too many variables affecting its outcome. In my previous solo climbs I had struggled with these same concerns and had overcome them, adding to my own sense of confidence, of identifying with the mountains and the natural environment. This trip felt more like a holiday: come to see, to be in the alpine environment, then, go back to my job in Delhi.

My uncertainty about Jean's situation didn't help. At least, I was in surroundings familiar to me. She was into a whole new space--nursing in a centre with minimal medical back-up, living in India for the first time. But like my decision to go to the mountains, she had accepted the challenge and the risks, deciding to work in the leper colony. Her new adventure was similar to my own foray. Each held a promise of excitement and learning, each held its dangers—individually and for our partnership. Regardless of our commitment to each other, we were each ultimately alone.

On our first full day in Harki Doon we hiked north through huge boulders, probably glacial erratics, strewn across the grassy floor of the valley, then east into a box-canyon, fenced by rock pinnacles soaring to 5000 metres. Here the sheep trails disappeared and the soft grass was replaced by gravel and, eventually, only rock. Angling up to the north ridge we climbed to a shoulder where we halted for lunch.

To the east we could see, beyond intervening ridges, two very high snowy peaks, perhaps Black Peak and Banderpunch, the latter over 6000 metres. Kulshan didn't recognize them, and the Indian government wouldn't sell me (or any other climber) maps for areas this close to the Chinese border! Farther up our ridge, a sharp rock peak beckoned. The route looked precarious with a section of fluted, knife-edged ice interrupting the long rock route. That one was impossible for us without crampons. Also, the day was half gone and I had already done enough, needing more time to acclimatize to the lack of oxygen. Kulshan started back to our camp while I settled on a rock to snap a panorama of photographs and to write my diary.

While not at all inaccessible, this valley probably had been visited by very few Westerners. We like to call these places "unexplored," but I sensed that Harki Doon had a long history, one that included animals and men living and dying in a dynamic, yet natural, equilibrium.

An hour later I was down by the creek in the canyon, tired and lethargic from the altitude and the tropical sun. The flowing water was ice-cold, but clear and inviting, if only for a ten second dip. Revitalised and fully awake, I dressed and walked down the meadow to our valley of the rocks. They looked great for boulder climbing and I tried several routes, toning finger strength, getting used to moving on steep rock. After one particularly difficult route, I hoisted on my hands to a mantle-shelf, gaining the flat top only to find

Kulshan smiling across from another rock about a hundred metres further along.

Dusk was upon us as we reached the tent and we quickly cooked up lentils and rice. Kulshan was a vegetarian, but I had packed some freeze-dried hamburger in the duffel bag. I dug it out, adding it to my own dish, warming the bland mixture.

Then it hit me. The meat had been with the barley sugars in the bottom of the bag when we left. Now it was near the top. Had Kulshan been into the bag? He hadn't. We started pulling food out, spreading it around on the ground. There was no candy left, none of the chocolate, tea, cheese!

"Rope?" Kulshan asked. We had left it in the very bottom. Inverting the sack, I shook out the dregs, but I knew it wasn't there.

"Damn those bastards!" I was mad. The shepherds had obviously come up to our camp, selectively gone through our gear, taken what they wanted and carefully repacked it. Could they believe that we wouldn't notice? We had given some candy to their kids on the way up from Osla! "Mattai!" they had called, a word all trekkers soon understand, "Candy!" Too late I realized our naivety.

"A bit of food is one thing, but the rope! They probably don't know how valuable it is. God, if they have cut it!" Kulshan seemed to understand my ranting.

"Where is the nearest police station?" I asked Kulshan when I had cooled down a few degrees. "Militia? You know, police? Are they in Osla?"

"In Taluka," he replied. "Tomorrow I scare them; they give rope back." But he didn't look all that confident. Through the long evening we planned what to do next day, how to find the shepherds, how to get back our rope. The robbery and the cold night brought us together. Kulshan baked little potatoes in the twig fire, more for something to do than for nourishment. Despite the lack of a common language, we were becoming friends. As our few twigs dwindled to embers, we rolled into our bags.

Before sun-up, Kulshan crossed the creek and headed for the big herd of sheep below us on the north bank. I followed about five minutes behind. He disappeared behind a huge boulder and did not reappear. I waited, then followed. As I rounded the corner, I quickly snapped several flash pictures of the shepherds, two still wrapped in their blankets and the headman stoking a small fire. Of course, they denied the theft. But Kulshan told them that they had until the next morning to replace the goods or we would report them to the Taluka policeman. They seemed to know what a camera was; Kulshan threatened to use the pictures as "proof."

We returned to the tent, had our breakfast and headed up the east tributary of the Supin River. All of our excess gear went into the tent and I snapped a small padlock on the door zipper. Anyone could slice the nylon and take it all. But we felt that our threats were understood.

Following a bench along the left ridge we walked north east, first along the edge of an expansive plateau of grass, then along an gravel strewn, crumbling glacier. Reaching the dogleg we followed the bank around for a few kilometres before stopping. To the north an open col led between granite spires; to the east a higher and icebound pass barred the way to Black Peak. Either of the routes could have provided several days of challenging climbing, of long fluted ice ridges and clean granite faces. But we would have needed an advance base camp to do them, more food and equipment and, probably, a stronger party.

While we munched our onions and cold potatoes, I gazed up through the notch leading towards Tibet, the border being about 40 kilometres further. I remembered Heinrich Harrer's incredible tale of escape from the British in Second World War India, of his solo journey northward into Tibet.

After the war he told his tale in *Seven Years in Tibet*, a story of reaching Lhasa, befriending and becoming advisor to the young Dalai Lama.

I guessed that this pass, being off the traditional trade routes, would have little surveillance. Part of me wanted that route, to go into the unknown, just to see where it would lead. But the permit stated clearly that I was forbidden to travel near the border. And I had told Jean I'd be back in two weeks, maximum. I could recall the same questioning I had done on Annapurna; this time I knew the answer without all the stress of longing.

We descended to the glacier and followed it down to the snout, never finding the melt water we sought. I should have known. Old glaciers are the same everywhere: irregular and rough to traverse, covered with unstable gravel piles, twice as long as you'd expect. Always, you can hear water splashing along several feet below the surface, just out of reach.

At the toe a dirty, crashing torrent emerged. We filtered some water for our canteens. The sun was warm, the grass soft. The valley was becoming familiar to me. Climbing back to the plateau, Kulshan spotted a grave, a raised earth mound ringed by specially chosen grey granite stones. It was strategically located, very old, and it blended into the meadow.

The grave was so unusual to my cultural ideas that it continued to run through my mind all afternoon as we followed the river as it slowed, crossing the open plain. Near the junction we left it, climbed up the hillside to our little fir forest. When we reached our camp, parched and beat, I turned and retraced our day's route. We could see the whole circuit except round the corner and up to my "Tibetan Col." I could still see the grave with its ring of stones at the top of the plateau, at the end of the good grazing.

"What a great place to die," I thought, "and even

better, what a place to be buried." I hoped that it was the grave of a shepherd, of a man who had spent his life in Harki Doon. So often, we bury our dead where there is no connection to their work or life. Primitive societies understand this so much better. They see death as a part of living, as the final great ceremony, but they assume that the spirit of the dead continues among them.

That night was even longer than the last and my mind was busy with all sorts of existential questions. Before first light I longed for the five o'clock summer mornings of Canada's latitudes. Perhaps I had my consciousness tuned for the footfall of a shepherd. I had given hardly a moment to thoughts of our missing rope. Kulshan seemed to sleep right through my wakefulness, but now he was stirring. I pulled on trousers and made a quick round of the camp. On the other side of the firepit, no more than ten paces from the tent, lay the rope, still coiled as I had stowed it in the duffel bag. There was no sign of the pilfered food.

When we left camp we took the rope with us. Kulshan led up the end of the south ridge through scrub brush on a shaded, north snow slope. It was very poor footing, a questionable line of ascent. But he was strong and acclimatized. And I wanted to get high. Even if this was merely a tourist trip, with no direction and no particular summit in mind, I needed to look around, especially east to Swargarohini and maybe even to Nanda Devi!

Eventually, Kulshan agreed to end his futile struggle and we traversed left, breaking through the snow crust every second step, wearing ourselves out. Around the next bluff the route laid back enough for the sun to warm it; the ground was visible in strips that led right up to the col connecting to the main ridge. By noon my altimeter indicated 4500 metres above sea level. The sun was nearly overhead, filtered by a smoke haze that permeated Harki Doon. The shepherds burned the grass each fall to promote rapid regrowth in the grassy valleys. But up on the ridge we were high enough to be cold, with the temperature just above freezing.

I felt I was finally in good shape. Kulshan was in better. He bounded ahead a hundred paces, then stopped with a grin while I grunted 25 paces, then hung over my iceaxe puffing for a count of ten, then did another 25, and so on up to the promontory. His high elevation home (and his relative youth) were starting to show.

We reached the snowfields at the saddle and roped up. To the right was the buttress Kulshan had tried to climb direct, to the left the first summit of the ridge. It was a moderate slope, inclined at thirty degrees, rising to the peak about 200 metres above us. But it took me nearly an hour to climb the snow slope. At the rock pile summit I collapsed, panting for several minutes before my heart reached a more normal cadence.

A series of pinnacles projected from the ridge, each one just a little higher, and behind them the clear formation of Black Peak, Swargarohini, and Banderpunch marching off to the east. From this perspective Kulshan named them off; on his training climb he had been up the Ruinsar Valley that now stretched below us. His excitement was apparent and, absorbing the sparkling panorama, we shared all of the elation of a more significant summit. It was only 5200 metres above sea level. But from its top we could see the whole of the ranges west, north and east. Lacking the shepherds' billowing smoke, we might have spied Nanda Devi. That day we could only imagine its faint white pyramid.

The descent, glissading down steep snow, was incredible. Skiing down the softened snow crust, using our ice axes as dragging brakes, we lost elevation so fast that our ears popped. In an hour we dropped off the snow patches into a stream bed in the valley. In another we were crossing the massive boulders that bridged the glacial torrent.

At the camp everything was in order. There had been no more visits from the thieves. In fact, all of the sheep had moved down the valley and we were totally alone in the calm evening. It seemed as though we had been in Harki Doon much longer that a few days. There still was much more to see, more to climb. The terrain was now familiar, the boulder field north of the camp, the ridge we had just come down, the little grave at the far end of the grass plateau.

That grave seemed to have a mystical hold on me. I wondered how I would approach death, whether I would accept it as a part of a sequence much longer and greater than my single life--not the end of all things. I had lost several friends in the mountains; I knew of other climbers who had died. Everyone knows of death, some see it daily in their professions. Alpinists have the opportunity to look at it in a premeditated way and know that it could occur as part of their unnecessary adventure.

With the coming of the nuclear age, authors have compared death to extinction and question if there is any difference. If I consider only *my* life to be significant, then death is equal to extinction. But when I approach my own death, I believe that my thoughts will be of my experience of life. That experience, with whatever contribution I imagine it represents, will have no meaning unless other human existence continues. It would be difficult to accept death as part of a world-ending conflagration. How much easier to accept death with equanimity, knowing it to be *a part* of my experience. I likened it to my past summits and sunrises, where I need to know that others will share these experiences.

In places like Harki Doon, I am struck by the logic of the lifestyle, by the simplicity, by the closeness of the people to each other and to nature. It reinforces for me the idea, prevalent also in trans-Himalayan cultures, of living a cycle where I am a part of a larger design. If I view life as having a clear beginning and end it is easy to disregard other people and species and to deal only with my personal well-being. But when I consider my life as a part of the whole existing world, including pre-history and the many generations that will follow, I feel more integrated and whole. While I am not likely to give up my own life easily or even my well-being, I may have more consideration for the world as an entity, for its systems, its species, each as having the same rights as I do.

In the East, reincarnation is an accepted concept, and one that I like. Despite its rational appeal, it is not yet a part of my belief structure. But more and more, I find it easy to consider myself as a part of a continuum, not merely a discrete entity with a definable lifetime. Primitive agricultural lifestyles make many of these ideas clearer.

That night we ate up everything, baking potatoes well into the dark. With all of my existential musings done, with my body well spent on our summit, I slept the sleep of the innocent.

We woke to a high overcast and immediately set to packing. After all of my initial troubles with kerosene--the first bottle leaking, the transfer to smaller ones, the oily stench permanently on my clothes--still I left half a litre at the forestry cabin rather than carry it down. We preferred a wood fire. Kulshan's potatoes needed baking and we needed the mesmerising force of a fire to draw us together, a focus where we could relax, pretend to do something, but do nothing.

Since the thieves had taken all of our fancy foods, we didn't need a porter and humped the remainder down ourselves. I piled more weight on Kulshan's pack--he hefted it with a laugh. All the way down to Sankri he explained to me that guides don't carry loads, porters do!

When the bus came the following morning we rode together to Mori where I hopped down. Kulshan was returning to Uttarkashi with a fist full of rupees and my promise to call him if I ever went to Nanda Devi.

I had only two hours to wait for my bus, but now I was impatient to get back to Dehra Doon, to share my trek with Jean, to hear of her experiences among the lepers. Amazingly, the bus arrived promptly and I relaxed into the seat (without any kerosene to worry about) for the eight hours of twisting roads and familiar spring-dead buses.

In front of me a young hill woman in a sari nursed a baby. To my unpractised eye the child looked no more than a few days old. Yet here they were, mother and daughter making their first trip, the start of their journey together. We were going down to the plains, down to the heat and dust of the plateau that is northern India.

"It is not incumbent upon you to complete the task, yet neither are you free to desist from it altogether."

Rabbi Tarphon, Talmud

The debris of winter storms lies everywhere on the dirty snow disguising the high-arched and frozen crust over the creek. The sun filters through the tops of the firs above White Pass, knifing down to the south bank of the gully. It warms the cool sea breeze funnelling up from below, sucking with it the memory of rotting mould and broken boughs from the forest floor. It warms also the reluctant snow patches and, as I pass, another chunk breaks off, collapses into the muddy torrent and dashes down, down and westward, past Mount Rainier to the Pacific.

I am on a long trail, one that extends from Mexico to Canada along the Coast ranges, sometimes on the ridges, sometimes through logging slash, usually somewhere between--in the high meadows above tree line. And I am travelling this, the Pacific Crest Trail, one that likely will occupy me for years.

Some hard hikers finish the whole 4200 kilometres in one season; about fifteen do it every year. They start at the Mexico border as early as possible, scheduling to be through the high Sierras of California early, but hoping not to be caught in spring storms. That is the high part of the trail, often reaching elevations of 3000 metres in the section also called the John Muir Trail. Then they hike through Oregon and past Mount Hood, averaging over 20 kilometres per day, nonstop! They must get through the Cascade Mountains of Washington before the November storms freeze them out while descending into Canada's Manning Park. For them, the Pacific Crest Trail is the ultimate challenge, one of physical endurance, but even more difficult, is the test of surviving five to six months, often alone.

"Gluttons for punishment," Dad would have called them, and maybe I will, too, before I'm done.

Just for now, I'm doing one section at a time. The one I'm on is only 155 kilometres. This project can last as long as I want it to, with side trips to other mountains, other continents. There should be no hurry this time. I am alone on the Trail, partly by choice, partly by the lack of available partners.

In a way this trip is like coming home to the Pacific Northwest and to my home in Canada. I see my time on the Trail, however many months or years it takes, as a spiritual rediscovery, a chance to remember and acknowledge the passage of events. In such a pilgrimage alone is better.

This journey, past Mount Rainier in Washington State and heading north to Canada, takes me within distant view of many mountains I've climbed: Mounts Hood, Olympus, Baker, Slesse, even Rainier itself. By starting this trek at White Pass and finishing somewhere near Glacier Peak, only a small part of the journey will be completed. Geographically, I should begin on the Mexican border or in Manning Park. But life's trail is equally undefined; it is no easy matter to say where one really began, what was the condition of personality or soul at the time of one's first climb. Memory is often inadequate, but nowhere less accurate than when viewing one's own attributes and faults.

Some days of a long trek are harder than others. It takes time to get used to a heavy pack and long hours on the trail. The views of Mounts Rainier and Adams are with me at every stop. The west provides the scenery and is the source of all the weather. Surprisingly, there are no hikers on this section over to Chinook Pass. It is devoid of human company. The deer pause in every swamp at my approach. And the nights are full of elk trumpeting.

The evening work of chores about the camp and the

need, while hiking, for alertness to follow the uncertain trail absorbs much of my attention. It is this pattern, this need to deal with life's daily essentials, that obscures progress. Change has come in my life in such irregular steps that it is difficult to detect the progression: flashes of awareness, separated by long months of (sometimes boring) living. On the trail it consists of carrying a pack and finding the route, campsite duties, like feeding myself, planning the next day's journey. There are similar tasks in the city.

Change is hard to measure at the time it happens. I can never see it coming, often find it is elusive, even in retrospect. Memory of adventures, physical events, climbs or treks like this one may be more accurate. But changes in my attitude toward my sport, my work, my relationships inside and outside of my family are possible to capture. And those kinds of change are easier for those close to me to detect.

Even with this spiritual myopia, I know that the mountains, and yoga, too, have had their influence on me. How could one travel these endless hills without expanding a connection with Nature? It grates my soul to witness the way the human race continues to manipulate and to destroy more and more natural phenomenon. Did it always? Perhaps humans were even less aware of their effect on other people, on nature, in the past. But now, our ability to destroy has technology behind it. Personally, I have grown to love our natural world, but more than that, now I feel I am a part of that world, both good and bad.

This halting integration of my life with the laws and spirit of nature can only have arisen from some integration of my own body, mind and spirit. It is the union defined by the term "yoga." I see the development of this admitted spirituality as having a direct link to my connection with nature. Whether or not I absorb the idea of an after-life or life on some other plane, I can, and do, accept the fact that my own death is an inconsequential event in terms of natural processes. What is important to me is what I can do now, in this life.

I cross the footbridge over Highway 410. The noise of humans has been with me since Dewey Lake, this being the weekend and many families are out in the woods. They are with me as I camp at Sheep Lake, but I use the mosquitoes as an excuse to stay in my tent. The netting cannot isolate me from the sharp reports of a youth shooting at fish in the lake. There are many campsites around and I can't identify which, if any, is home to his parents.

In the morning I lose most of the weekend campers and look forward to a week before the next encounter with highway "civilization." Later I meet a woman coming up from Crystal Mountain Ski Area leading a llama carrying packs on each side. We talk briefly while the llama ogles me. It is a fascinating animal--gentle, perhaps even skittish--but inquisitive. Its intelligent eyes looked right *at* me.

They do not prevent me from a navigation error. I take the wrong fork, wind up on another trail to the west side of the ridge that obviously leads down to the ski basin. The error costs me four miles, an hour and a half climbing back over the spine. But no more people that day or the next. Near Camp Ulrich I see a string of horses coming down the trail. As they close I see four riders and two pack animals, so I move to the side to let them pass. The leader pauses to speak but at that moment the trailing rider hollers "hornets!" and whacks the flank of his pony. They all gallop south, leaving me to deal with the nest they have stirred up. Fortunately, I am far enough off the trail to miss the hornets' pursuit and I exaggerate the separation by a wide loop around the nest.

The next day I climb the long rise to Blowout Mountain, short of water but fearing rain. The clouds are blowing over the ridge crest, curling into fog on the lee side. I am clear of the drenching fog but hurry down to a pond below the summit in time to set up my tent against the rain, which starts the moment I am in. I cook lentils and rice under the fly and settle in for a long evening.

This is a different trip for me. I have been solo before, but not looking at a destination that is so indefinite. I don't expect to finish the entire Pacific Crest Trail for years, or even make the Canadian border for a while. Maybe this is an indication of progress of a sort. I am less interested in the end result, more fixed on the journey. This change is one that happens naturally with increasing age; you lose the fearlessness of youth, experiences of near-disasters accumulate, leading to a more conservative approach. The longer treks take time which is not available to you while holding down a regular job, while raising a family of young children.

But I have also made a conscious choice, a decision to avoid some of the polar opposites: success or failure, anticipation or disappointment, and many others. Most are tied to ego, most relate to my own picture of myself. The introspection that comes with many miles of solo travel has its value. There are few activities that allow memory its full rein, allow each adventure, each relationship, to be examined with the detailed perspective of time. But the awareness gained through time has started to remove my clouds of ego, and mists of personality. Can I now see what actually was happening?

It is possible to think, in a detached way, about my personal philosophy. The question is, "does this actually change my personality, the way I interact with other people?" Each adventure has an impact on me, on Jean's life and on our life together. My sister used to call it "parallel growth," that need for partners always to be pursuing and perfecting their own interests, but not always in the same field. That works for us. There is certainly a lower stress level in our relationship now than at the start. I can credit Jean more than me, yoga more than mountaineering. My yoga is nothing more (or less) than a conscious awareness of self and surroundings. Without it, mountaineering is just climbing big rocks. With the awareness brought by yoga, my mountain passages have formed a physical link to the whole of my world and a psychic connection to my own spirituality.

Life analogies, with or without the symbolism of yoga asanas, are ever present. They can be ignored or denigrated as amusing coincidences. Or they can form a platform for real learning. Practically speaking, this Pacific Crest Trail has no end for me, no summit to be reached, no paramount panorama to be viewed. It is a process, a journey. I recognize my new tendency toward this kind of adventure. The summits still have their appeal, but the reasons have changed.

The world will have a limited memory of me in a century, or even a decade, after my death. My life, my contribution, really has little significance to future generations. I fully accept the continuity of life and it is easier to see that Buddhist point of view. My work really *is* for me and my own development, *not* for the world. The reasons for doing the work and the importance of its quality and completeness are still valid parts of the work. But the learning exercise for me is as significant as any benefit to the community. The cup has finally emptied and I can refill it. How did it become empty, how did I become receptive to that lesson? I wonder which occurred first, the thought of life as a never-ending process or my actual living of it that way.

The onion soup is finally boiling. That's the only treat I've got left now. It will be cornmeal, rice, and lentils until Snoqualmie Pass. Still a long day to get to the pass. I hope it's all in standing timber and not logged.

Fresh blueberries were the only attraction of this day's part of the Trail. I've traversed at least 30 kilometres of forest recently clear-cut. The route was sometimes eliminated, often obscured. There were new-growth blueberry bushes encroaching on the path, soaking me after two days of rain. Strangely, after several days alone, around noon I met three travellers all at once. John and Neil from New Zealand were heading south. They appeared very heavily-laden, yet neither dropped his pack while we compared notes on the route ahead. They were obviously fit; their systems looked more comfortable than mine. I welcomed the chance to drop my cruiser frame even though its weight is now less than twenty kilograms. They told me about a great "bed-and-breakfast" where I can stay at Snoqualmie Pass.

While we were talking, Andy Selters trotted up the path, arriving with questions, especially about the newly-logged "disaster" zones. He is co-author of the guide book I'm using, and is checking out trail changes for a revised edition. If I had expected to meet the author I would have kept better notes.

The "Kiwi's" then continued southward while Andy and I came north to this creek. Now, despite the late hour and the three kilometres back to his half-ton we talk like old friends. My need to converse is obvious. Andy wants to know more about northern India. He's got a permit to climb Rhimo III in the southern part of the Karakorum Range. Border hostilities may prevent his team from entering the area. My friend Dilsher from Dehra Doon may be able to help sort out the difficulties with the Indian Mountaineering Federation. The Rhimo massif is only 180 kilometres north of Srinagar, where I worked on a hospital solar heating system. I tell Andy about hiking near the Pakistan border.

"In a few months, I'll be there myself," he smiles, and hitches to leave. Andy's book makes this trip simpler for me and many other trekkers. Every traveller can assist those who follow. Dilsher can assist Andy in the Karakorum; first ascent climbers do make subsequent climbs easier by the very fact that you know the route is possible.

On the early climbs in my youth, pitons driven into rock cracks provided security against a fall--a safer environment for the risk-taking of climbing. Some took it too far. They could place "bolts" all the way up an otherwise inaccessible peak. We called it "nailing" up a cliff you could not otherwise dream of climbing.

There are many "crutches" we use to support our special wilderness activities: a route description from someone who has been there before, a donkey to carry our load, sometimes a helicopter ferry into a remote region, even the pitons and other devices that support our confidence. Each of us has to decide what life will consist of, how we will live it, what chances we will take. Our experiences in one situation will invariably influence how the next mountain will be climbed, how the next journey will be travelled. All activities we take seriously provide us with tools for exploring awareness, understanding ourselves and our surroundings. All can become conscious worship if we can find the "guru-within," the self-teacher.

This section of the Trail is nearly ended, the last day by far the hardest. Even with a lightened load, my shoulders are tired from the straps, my feet sore with the pounding. Above Interstate 90 my path follows the roar of vehicles pouring over Snoqualmie Pass from Seattle. Past Lodge Lake I start to meet hikers, families out for the day. I am happy that many have young children along, that they are clearly enjoying the outing. At Beaver Lake I start the final descent, down the long, grassy hill under the lifts that haul skiers in winter. I can see the little village across the highway where the New Zealanders found the "bed and breakfast." My whole body could use a rest. There'll be a telephone there, too.

Andy's guidebook says the next part of the Trail is higher, tougher, but even more inspiring. From here, Guye Peak looks spectacular; Red Mountain is obviously higher than the peaks on this side of the highway. The Pacific Crest Trail traverses just east of them, seems to follow a series of ridges, truly an alpine crest.

But first, I'm in need of "psychic decompression." Tomorrow, a week or a year from now, I'll continue the Trail up the other side.

With thirty years in the mountains, Gil Parker had myriad adventures and many rope partners. He was Vice-President of the Alpine Club of Canada, 1976-1980.

While studying at Yasodhara Ashram in south-east British Columbia, he began recording the similarities of the personal challenges faced in climbing and in the yogic life.

An engineer by training, a writer by choice, Gil has served the World Federalists, the Solar Energy Society, the Victoria School of Writing. The Rotary Club awarded him a Fellowship for introducing Rotary in Russia. He is an Honorary Citizen of the City of Victoria.

ISBN 155212965-9

9 781552 129654